D0765424

We Have Never Been Middle Class

First published by Verso 2019
© Hadas Weiss 2019

The moral rights of the author have been asserted

1 3 5 7 9 10 8 6 4 2

Verso
UK: 6 Meard Street, London W1F 0EG
US: 20 Jay Street, Suite 1010, Brooklyn, NY 11201
versobooks.com

Verso is the imprint of New Left Books

ISBN-13: 978-1-78873-391-5
ISBN-13: 978-1-78873-393-9 (UK EBK)
ISBN-13: 978-1-78873-394-6 (US EBK)

British Library Cataloguing in Publication Data
A catalogue record for this book is available from the British Library

Library of Congress Cataloging-in-Publication Data

Names: Weiss, Hadas, author.
Title: We have never been middle-class / Hadas Weiss.
Description: London ; Brooklyn, NY : Verso, 2019. | Includes
   bibliographical references and index.
Identifiers: LCCN 2019018761 (print) | LCCN 2019981033 (ebook) | ISBN
   9781788733915 | ISBN 9781788733939 (UK EBK) | ISBN 9781788733946 (US
   EBK)
Subjects: LCSH: Middle class. | Social classes.
Classification: LCC HT684 .W45 2019 (print) | LCC HT684 (ebook) | DDC
   305.5/5—dc23
LC record available at https://lccn.loc.gov/2019018761
LC ebook record available at https://lccn.loc.gov/2019981033

Typeset in Fournier by Biblichor Ltd, Edinburgh
Printed and bound by CPI Group (UK) Ltd, Croydon CR0 4YY

We Have Never Been Middle Class

Hadas Weiss

VERSO

Contents

Acknowledgments:
The Middle Class (A Love Story)

As an anthropologist, I have always been my first informant. The ideas in this book emerge out of challenges I confronted in my adult life, but even more so out of nostalgia for the values I was brought up with. Many people have kept these values alive against countervailing evidence by facilitating and rewarding my work, and I am now in the happy position of being able to acknowledge their contribution.

For reasons of confidentiality I cannot name the individual subjects of my fieldwork, so I will express my deep collective gratitude to the Israelis and Germans whose generosity in interviews and in allowing me to observe their interactions made my research possible.

I am incredibly fortunate to have been trained at the University of Chicago's Department of Anthropology, where every professor I had was an inspiration. Jean Comaroff, John Kelly and Moishe Postone guided my endeavors in dissertation writing and far beyond. Jean's support over the years, in particular, was vital for my career and peace of mind. Moishe congratulated me on the upcoming publication of this book and it breaks my heart that he passed away before I could gift him a copy. John Comaroff and Susan Gal offered help at crucial points and Anne Chien made everything easier. Thanks also to the friends who have made Chicago my home away from home: Michael Bechtel, Rachel-Shlomit Brezis, Michael Cepek, Jason Dawsey, Abigail Dean, Jennifer Dowler, Amanda Englert, Yaqub Hilal, Lauren Keeler, Tal Liron, Sarah Luna, Elayne Oliphant, Alexis Salas, Noa Vaisman, Eitan Wilf, Rodney Wilson and Tal Yifat.

At Frankfurt's Goethe University, Hans Peter Hahn was a great supervisor. I thank him and my friends there: Jennifer Bagley, Vitali Bartash, Federico Buccellati, Gordana Ciric, Tobias Helms, Kristin Kastner, Harry Madhathil, Mario Schmidt and Walburga Zumbroich. At the Helsinki Collegium for Advanced Studies, I learned so much from Turo-Kimmo Lehtonen and Joel Robbins. I am grateful to them and to Sorin Gog, Sarah Green, Simo Muir, Nadia Nava, Saara Pallander, Minna Ruckenstein, Filip Sikorsky, José Filipe Silva and Andras Szigeti for brightening up the winters. At Central European University's Institute for Advanced Study in Budapest, Eva Fodor was the perfect director. I thank her and Duane Corpis, Thomas Paster, Craig Roberts, James Rutherford, Kai Schafft and Julianne Werlin for being the first to express enthusiasm about ideas that would make it into this book. At the Max Planck Institute for Social Anthropology in Halle, Chris Hann and Don Kalb sat me down to write it and offered encouragement along the way. I thank them and the colleagues who made me happy to come into the office: Saskia Abrahms-Kavunenko, Tristam Barrett, Charlotte Bruckermann, Natalia Buier, Dimitra Kofti, Marek Mikuš, Sylvia Terpe and Samuel Williams.

My Leipzig sojourn breezed by thanks to Moran Aharoni, Nora Gottlieb, Agathe Mora and Jon Schubert. Life in Berlin was more play than work thanks to Guy Gilad, Andreas Markowsky, Katarzyna Puzon, André Thiemann, Alina Vaisfeld, Roberta Zavoretti and Gabriele Zipf. Academic nomadism won me precious friendships with Ivan Ascher, Paul Daniel, Rotem Geva, Ehud Halperin, Matan Kaminer, Patrick Neveling, Dimitris Sotiropoulos and Christian Stegle. Back in Israel, my oldest friends Nira Ben-Aliz, Tzipi Berman, Tsahala Samet and Nitsa Zafrir reminded me of what matters. I thank them all from the bottom of my heart.

Ivan Ascher, Josh Berson, Charlotte Bruckermann, Mateusz Halawa, Yoav Halperin, Yaqub Hilal, Marek Mikuš, Eckehart Stamer and Mordechai Weiss read part or full drafts of this book and gave me excellent suggestions. For Verso, Sebastian Budgen and Richard Seymour did the same. I am grateful to them and in particular to Amanda Englert, always my most brilliant and painstaking reader.

I want to acknowledge the journals from which I paraphrased portions of my previously published work: "Homeownership in Israel: The Social Costs of Middle-Class Debt," *Cultural Anthropology* 2014, vol. 29(1): 128–49; "Capitalist Normativity: Value and Values," *Anthropological Theory* 2015, vol. 15(2): 239–53; "Contesting the Value of Household Property," *Dialectical Anthropology* 2016, vol. 40(3): 287–303; "Longevity Risk: A Report on the Banality of Finance Capitalism," *Critical Historical Studies* 2018, vol. 5(1): 103–9; and "Lifecycle Planning and Responsibility: Prospection and Retrospection in Germany," *Ethnos* 2019.

My brother, Tal Weiss, and my sister, Lilach Weiss, were always there to cheer me on. My nephews and nieces, Shachar,

Aviv, Yuval, Tomer, Michael, Yaara and Avigail, added sweetness and joy. Neither this book nor anything else I have ever accomplished would have been possible without the unconditional love and steadfast support of my parents, Rachel and Mordechai Weiss. Words cannot express the depth of my love and gratitude for my wonderful family.

Introduction:

We Have Never Been Middle Class

The middle class does not exist. For all the time we spend talking about it, much of what we say is contradictory. We worry about its decline or squeeze: that there are fewer people today who can consider themselves middle class than there were a mere decade ago and that, the way things are going, those who are on the brink will soon fall over the edge. But we are also cheered by headlines suggesting that if we only think globally, we will discover that the middle class is actually on the rise, its ranks swelling with go-getting pursuers of happiness in places like China, India, Brazil and South Africa. In one of those old tricks of language, at the same time that we question the numbers of people who are middle class, we affirm the notion that there is a middle class out there for people to climb into or drop out of.

There isn't. One way to tell is by looking at studies conducted over the years to identify members of the middle class. Flip through research and analysis papers published by policy and consulting firms, think tanks, development agencies, marketing agencies, government agencies and central banks, and you find as many criteria as outcomes. Statisticians are particularly hard pressed to come up with universally applicable measurements. People in wealthy countries enjoy standards of living, work and consumption that the vast majority of the world population can only dream of, including those most likely to be identified as among the brave new global middle classes. What possible classification can encompass them all?

There are many possible groupings. Occupation is one: counting as middle class all manner of skilled professionals, managers and experts, and just about anyone else who performs nonmanual labor. It is temptingly intuitive until you think about the multitudes of underemployed and struggling white-collar professionals or, conversely, about high-earning nonprofessionals who just as intuitively defy the classification. Another popular criterion is relative immunity to poverty: deeming middle class those people who have sufficient resources to protect them against imminent hunger or want. But here again, we have all heard horror stories of upstanding members of the middle class abruptly toppled from riches to rags by personal, national and global market crises. Some analysts look at levels of disposable income, reading as middle class any earners whose incomes exceed, by a fixed measure, what would be required for the daily upkeep of their household and who can therefore buy nonnecessities. This definition misleadingly assumes steady incomes from which expenses can be computed and fixed portions parceled out in a world in which money actually flows in and out of households in highly irregular fashion. Other analysts define middle classes by absolute income levels. They face similar problems and then some, even when adjusting for national price indexes. The relative value of money is one thing; quite another is what people can do with it given the local material and social infrastructure and the political circumstances with which they contend. People enjoying comparable income levels in different countries have living standards so radically different from one another that it is hard to imagine them belonging to the same group. Still others define the middle class as middle income: those occupying the median of a country's income brackets. This makes cross-country comparisons impossible, and besides, in each country there is too little variance between middle and somewhat lower income brackets to convincingly distinguish their members from one another. The most interesting criterion is what hard-nosed quantitative analysts call the subjective one: simply asking people to label themselves. It always trips analysts up because, by and large, many more people self-identify as middle class than would be so identified by any of the other criteria. This is true just about everywhere in the world and applies to those who would otherwise be considered both above and below the designated middle.[1]

---

1 A. V. Banerjee and E. Duflo, "What Is the Middle Class About? The Middle Classes Around the World," *MIT Discussion Papers*, December 2007; R. Burger, S. Kamp, C. Lee, S. van der Berg, and A. Zoch, "The Emergent Middle Class in Contemporary South Africa: Examining and Comparing Rival Approaches," *Development South Africa*, 2015, 32(1), 24–40; D. Kalb, "Class," in D. M. Nonini, ed., *A Companion to Urban Anthropology* (New York: Blackwell, 2014); C. L. Kerstenetzky, C. Uchôa, and N. do Valle Silva, "The Elusive New Middle Class in Brazil," *Brazilian Political Science Review*, 2015, 9(3); H. Koo, "The Global Middle Class: How Is It Made, What Does It Represent?," *Globalizations*, 2016, 13(3); H. Melber, ed., *The Rise of Africa's Middle Class: Myths, Realities, and Critical Engagements* (London: Zed Books, 2016); M. Nundee, *When Did We All Become Middle Class?* (London: Routledge, 2016); G. M. D. Dore, "Measuring the Elusive Middle Class and Estimating Its Role in Economic

If analysts are diffident about defining the middle class, representatives of the public and business sectors have no such qualms. Pundits exhibit broad consensus in finding the middle class to be a really good thing, invariably deploring its squeeze and celebrating its growth. The so-called middle class is also the darling of politicians left and right, conservative and liberal, all claiming to represent middle-class interests with the policies they promote. Think tanks and consulting firms help political actors appeal to self-identified or aspirational middle classes. While they come up with strategies to expand the middle class, marketers guide corporate executives on how to cater to middle-class fantasies. Joining forces with professional literature and reportage, these actors associate the middle class with a host of social and economic desirables. In particular, they single out security, consumerism, entrepreneurship and democracy as middle-class mainstays. They further represent these attributes as interconnected, one leading naturally to the other in a virtuous cycle of economic growth, modernization and collective well-being.[2]

Development and Democracy," *World Economics Journal*, 2017, 18(2), 107–22; G. Therborn, "Class in the Twenty-First Century," *New Left Review*, 2012, 78 (November–December), 5–29. All of these provide critical summaries of many of these approaches, which are used more liberally and optimistically in such studies as S. Drabble, S. Hoorens, D. Khodyakov, N. Ratzmann, and O. Yaqub, "The Rise of the Global Middle Class: Global Social Trends to 2030," *Rand Corporation, Thematic Report 6*, 2015; and the "IMF: Global Financial Stability Report: Market Developments and Issues," International Monetary Fund, September 2006.

2   For example, in G. Amoranto, N. Chun and A. Deolaliker, "Who Are the Middle Class and What Values Do They Hold? Evidence from the World Values Survey," *Asian Development Bank Working Paper Series*, 2010, no. 229; C. Jaffrelot and P. van der Veer, eds., *Patterns of Middle Class Consumption in India and China* (London: Sage, 2012); M. Doepke and F. Zilibotti, "Social

Meanwhile, social scientists who have bothered to examine the lives of people who are presumed to be part of the new global middle classes cast serious doubt on each of these attributes. They describe populations united not by prosperity but by nagging insecurity, indebted ownership and compulsive overwork. They report on the inclination of these people to hoard what extra cash they have or to invest it toward things like a home or insurance rather than spending their disposable income on consumer goods. They identify their preferences for regular wages, whenever they can find them, over risky entrepreneurial profits, the pursuit of which is more often a forced adjustment to the absence of steady employment. And they underline their political pragmatism in backing whatever parties and policies might protect their interests rather than offering blanket support for democracy: something that is easy to spot in the recent history of Latin America and in present-day China.[3]

Class and the Spirit of Capitalism," *Journal of the European Economic Association*, 2005, 3(2–3), 516–24; S. Drabble, S. Hoorens, D. Khodyakov, N. Ratzmann and O. Yaqub, "The Rise of the Global Middle Class: Global Social Trends to 2030," *Rand Corporation*, *Thematic Report 6*, 2015; N. Eldaeva, O. Khakhlova, O. Lebedinskaya and E. Sibirskaya, "Statistical Evaluation of Middle Class in Russia," *Mediterranean Journal of Social Sciences*, 2015, 6(3), 125–34; S. D. Johnson and Y. Kandogan, "The Role of Economic and Political Freedom in the Emergence of Global Middle Class," *International Business Review*, 2016, 25(3), 711–25; C. L. Lufumpa and M. Ncube, *The Emerging Middle Class in Africa* (New York: Routledge, 2016); as well as any popular magazine you happen to pick up. One failed attempt to define the middle class concludes that it is extremely important for democracy, economy and society, despite the impossibility of defining it: T. Billitteri, "Middle Class Squeeze," *CQ Press*, 2009, 9–19.

3   Some of these issues have been identified among "the Western middle classes" by L. Chauvel and A. Hartung, "Malaise in the Western Middle Classes," *World Social Science Report 2016*, 164–69, as well as a range of

This is to say that "middle class" is an exceptionally nebulous category, neither clearly demarcated nor convincingly positive. Yet its vagueness in no way stops it from being

non-Western middle classes by Banerjee and Duflo, "What Is the Middle Class About? The Middle Classes Around the World"; R. Burger, M. Louw, B. B. I. de Oliveira Pegado and S. van der Berg, "Understanding Consumption Patterns of the Established and Emerging South African Black Middle Class," *Development South Africa* 2015, 32(1), 41–56; J. Chen, *A Middle Class without Democracy: Economic Growth and the Prospects of Democratization in China* (Oxford: Oxford University Press, 2013); S. Cohen, *Searching for a Different Future* (Durham: Duke University Press, 2004); A. Duarte, "The Short Life of the New Middle Class in Portugal," *International Research Journal of Arts and Social Science*, 2016, 3(2), 47–57; A. R. Embong, *State Led Mobilization and the New Middle Class in Malaysia* (London: Palgrave Macmillan, 2002); L. Fernandes, *India's New Middle Class* (Minneapolis: University of Minnesota Press, 2006); D. James, "'Deeper into a Hole?'" Borrowing and Lending in South Africa," *Current Anthropology* 55(S9), 17–29; D. James, *Money for Nothing: Indebtedness and Aspiration in South Africa* (Stanford: Stanford University Press, 2015); H. Koo, "The Global Middle Class: How Is It Made, What Does It Represent?"; M. MacLennan and B. J. Margalhaes, eds., "Poverty in Focus," *Bureau for Development Policy (UNDP)*, 2014, 26; H. Melber, *The Rise of Africa's Middle Class: Myths, Realities, and Critical Engagements*; J. Osburg, *Anxious Wealth: Money and Morality Among China's New Rich* (Stanford: Stanford University Press, 2013); B. P. Owensby, *Intimate Ironies: Modernity and the Making of Middle-Class Lives in Brazil* (Stanford: Stanford University Press, 1999); J. L. Rocca, *The Making of the Chinese Middle Class: Small Comfort and Great Expectations*, The Sciences Po Series in International Relations and Political Economy 2017; M. Shakow, *Along the Bolivian Highway: Social Mobility and Political Culture in a New Middle Class* (Philadelphia: University of Pennsylvania Press, 2014); J. Sumich, "The Uncertainty of Prosperity: Dependence and the Politics of Middle-Class Privilege in Maputo," *Ethnos*, 2015, 80(1), 1–21; A. Sumner and F. B. Wietzke, "What Are the Political and Social Implications of the 'New Middle Classes' in Developing Countries?" *International Development Institute Working Paper 3*, 2014; M. van Wessel, "Talking about Consumption: How an Indian Middle Class Dissociates from Middle-Class Life," *Cultural Dynamics*, 2004, 16(1), 93–116; and C. Freeman, R. Heiman and M. Liechty, eds., *Charting an Anthropology of the Middle Classes* (Santa Fe: SAR Press, 2012).

mobilized across the board. The concept holds immense trans-national popularity expressed not only in pronouncements by political and economic leaders about middle-class interests, virtues and aspirations, but also in the eagerness of people from all walks of life, all over the world, to identify themselves as members of the middle class. Now, when an anthropologist comes across a category so highly esteemed yet so poorly defined, and when she sees this category nevertheless deployed so vigorously by politicians, development agencies, corporate actors and marketing experts, she is likely to think of one thing: ideology.

In studying a host of issues popularly associated with the middle class in Israel and Germany while taking occasional sidelong glances at their global counterparts, I found this ideology everywhere. It prompted me to become more direct in questioning how the people I was observing were identi-fied. If in fact the middle class is an ideology, I asked myself, what does it mean? What purpose does it serve? How did it come about and what makes it so compelling? This book is my way of answering these questions and exploring their implications.

I address the arguments in it, idiosyncratically enough, to an implicated readership. This calls for explanation. In this day and age, the pronoun "we" is suspect and almost always calls forth a defiant "not-me." All manner of politicians, bosses, pas-tors and activists bandy it about to rally heterogeneous publics for causes they declare to be common. "We" is pronounced more spontaneously in opposition to the "not-we," whether a powerful 1 percent to our 99 or a counterpublic perceived as threatening who we are and what we have. What I have in mind here is inclusiveness of a different kind, neither superimposed nor collectively proclaimed for strategic purposes or against a supposed opposition. It is rather a quiet, self-congratulatory "we," which underscores a conceit of ours.

Sociologist Bruno Latour wrote *We Have Never Been Modern* to counter one such conceit: the view we have of ourselves as modern, or not primitive, in touting an objectivity based on separating the human from the nonhuman, the social world from the natural one. Latour claimed that such separation never really existed and considered hybrids like global warming, data banks and biotechnology as defying the belief that it ever has. Salient as this presumption is, he argued, it is a Western scientific and industrial construct. He proceeded to relativize it by elaborating on a prehistory and a posterity in which its absence is evident.

Thanks to Latour's trailblazing work, I never questioned whether I could argue similarly against the conceit of the middle class. I believe the category to be false in that it suggests powers that we do not possess. I also believe it to be ideological in that it invokes these powers for purposes that are not our own and whose consequences are not to our benefit. But I did struggle with addressing this argument to an implicated readership. If there is one thing that an anthropologist is allergic to, it is universalizing: assuming all too easily that the way I imagine myself to be right now is the way we all are and always have been by gift of nature, decree of god or the manifestation of some innate instinct. Anthropologists have traditionally studied not "us" but "them," that is, people who do things differently and whose otherness resists knee-jerk generalizations. A book written for and about us is therefore counterintuitive for an anthropologist.

But I made this choice deliberately, because one thing

that does fall squarely within the domain of anthropology is critique. Anthropology's fascination with all things remote and foreign does not normally feign a neutral, scientific or objective gaze as in the likes of *National Geographic*. To the contrary, it has often been a means through which to make some meaningful intervention in the distinctions and attributes people take to be universal, all those mundane assumptions that are nearby and familiar, whether about the nature and veracity of race and ethnic distinctions; the sources and consequences of gender roles and sexual preferences; the boundaries and peculiarities of childhood, adolescence, adulthood and old age; the social uses of beliefs, rituals, emotions and scientific reasoning; the patterns and functions of eating, working, leisure and sleep; the definitions and significance of health and pathology; the relations that make up families, tribes and nation states—and the list goes on.

The logic goes something like this. If somewhere out there people behave in ways that are, for example, neither egoistic nor self-serving, then people's self-serving behaviors in the advanced capitalist economies that most anthropologists come from and in which they disseminate their findings must stem from something other than an innate human disposition. Or if people elsewhere in the world succeed, for example, in satisfying their needs and desires with more egalitarian or collectively managed organizations for the production and distribution of goods and services, there are imaginable alternatives to our own economic and political systems.

The challenge of critique has grown more complicated, however, with the contraction of anthropology's traditional terrain. The far reaches of the world are no longer so distant, and societies once foreign and exotic have long been drawn into the global networks of market and media. Critically minded anthropologists find themselves at an impasse. On the one hand, they are motivated to upend overhasty assumptions, debunk complacent generalizations and trouble entrenched structures of domination. On the other, they are just as entangled as the people they study in an elaborate and comprehensive social and economic web that—in the competitive pressures it imposes, the self-concern it generates and the penalties and incentives it introduces into everyone's work, consumption and relationships—is all but universal. This leaves them hard pressed to find a standpoint from which to criticize forces that affect them as much as their subjects.

Anthropologists who have done so successfully have mostly focused on populations of the global peripheries that, while being subject to the pressures of global capitalism, lead lives that are partly removed from it. Yet even these populations are now fully entangled in the global production and circulation of money and commodities, regulated through institutions established or updated to channel their flow. These institutions include nation-states, the nuclear family, the free market, credit and debt, private property, human capital, investment and insurance. Each possesses its own rationale, which—because it is insuperably entwined with all others in the world we have created—seems so essential that it is hard to think of it as something that people have developed and tweaked at certain points in time to contend with or manipulate the conditions in which they found themselves. Such institutions appear wherever capitalism takes hold. They shape the way people understand themselves, whether as employees, investors, debtors, citizens, family members, property owners or members of a social class. The universalizing thrust implied by "we" is therefore neither whimsical nor presumptuous but a by-product of the ubiquity of capitalism itself.

Capitalism's universalization is most conspicuous with respect to the category of the middle class because this category is extensive and inclusive to the core: it projects an image of every human being as a self-determining investor of money, time or effort, if not at this very moment then in potential and aspiration. It imagines society to be a composite of multiple interacting individuals who are willing to exert more effort than they are immediately rewarded for, shoulder a greater debt burden than they absolutely must, and scale back on expenses whenever they can, in order to build reserves for their future and for that of their families. The fortunes of all but those who are deprived of the means to invest in this way due to various social and geographical barriers that these people are presumably in the process of overcoming, are thereupon considered the outcome of their personal investments.

The image of an expansive and increasingly global middle class that everyone could join does away with such divisive categories as workers vs. capitalists, unless it implies that deep down everyone is a quasi-capitalist go-getter. It also softens the edges of other potentially divisive categories like gender, ethnicity, race, nationality and religion, to the extent that middle-class alliances and competitions are designed to cut through and transcend the boundaries that these divisions lay down, inviting people to redefine their place in society according to their private interests.[4] It embraces diversity insofar as manifold distinctions are validated and identities made to

---

4 Although anthropologists have shown that when the category of middle class gets entangled with ethnic, religious and gendered attributes, it

flourish through the range of consumer items that more and more people can access. At the same time, it exacerbates inequality by encouraging competitive consumption, lifestyle and investment to signal advantages for some over others and to guard against disadvantages relative to others.

Middle classness implies that we take responsibility over our fortunes by working as best as we can while forgoing some immediate enjoyment as we cut back on our expenses (and while sacrificing some peace of mind as we borrow to finance the purchase of durable assets) in order to be rewarded for these forfeitures in the future. It implies that our misfortunes are consequently a result of our having made poor or insufficient use of the time, energy and resources at our disposal; that society is nothing but a plethora of individuals implicated in each others' self-serving investments, sometimes as allies and sometimes as competitors; and that its institutions are realizations of working investors' respective or combined powers and preferences.

---

can sharpen their boundaries. See, for example, X. Zang, "Socioeconomic Attainment, Cultural Tastes, and Ethnic Identity: Class Subjectivities among Uyghurs in Ürümchi," *Ethnic and Racial Studies*, 2016; Burger et al., "The Emergent Middle Class in Contemporary South Africa: Examining and Comparing Rival Approaches"; H. Donner, *Domestic Goddesses: Modernity, Globalisation, and Contemporary Middle-Class Identity in Urban India* (London: Routledge, 2008); C. Freeman, "The 'Reputation' of 'Neoliberalism,'" *American Ethnologist*, 2007, 34(2), 252–67; A. Maqsood, *The New Pakistani Middle Class* (Cambridge, Mass: Harvard University Press, 2017); C. Jones, "Women in the Middle: Femininity, Virtue, and Excess in Indonesian Discourses of Middle-Classness," in R. Heiman, C. Freeman and M. Liechty, eds., *The Middle Classes: Theorizing through Ethnography* (Santa Fe: School for Advanced Research Press, 2012); and A. Ricke, "Producing the Middle Class: Domestic Tourism, Ethnic Roots, and Class Routes in Brazil," *The Journal of Latin American and Caribbean Anthropology*, 2017.

If we identify with these ideas, or if, more commonly, we express them unreflectingly in our behaviors and sensibilities, it is because they are built into the very rhythms of our lives, into the instruments we deploy and into the institutions through which our activities are organized. It is also because sometimes they are in fact affirmed by provisional and relative rewards when larger investors acquire advantages over lesser ones, as do, for example, landlords over tenants. But if we have misgivings, they likely awaken when the instruments we use and the institutions we operate within no longer function quite so smoothly, and when the rewards suggested by investment-driven self-determination are not forthcoming. Philosopher G. W. F. Hegel famously wrote that the owl of Minerva spreads its wings with the falling of dusk, by which he meant that we are prone to understand things only after the fact. In this case, the hour of critique chimes at the dusk of the middle-class ideal, when a chorus of voices laments its decline. The timing, as I will explain in this book, has everything to do with the growing dominance in recent decades of global finance. Finance's dominance exports middle-class identifications into newly liberalized economies while at the same time squeezing household resources in countries whose populations have long been considered predominantly middle class.

I hope, then, that my decision to address an inclusive "we" in this book will not be taken as a sign of my ignorance of or disrespect for real differences between people. I know and appreciate that there are many people who live under vastly different conditions, people unable to command resources and lacking the potential to fare better (or worse) as the result of their investments, people who share none of the premises upon which this book is based. Rather, this form of address emerges out of my determination to take seriously the structural forces that have generated and popularized the image of a porous and expansive middle class and rendered it plausible. My intention is to pick apart this plausibility for those to whom it applies, for example those who are inclined to read this book. I do assume that, like me, you are products of some investment in education, if in nothing else—that you dedicate time and money to learn more and that you implicitly believe in the long-term significance of these endeavors. Speaking directly to a readership that makes investments of this kind, I hope to tap into something else we have in common: the proclivity to reflect on our received wisdoms.

With more of us out there insecure and struggling despite the prudent investments we have made and continue to make for our future, the promises of the middle class no longer seem so credible, and the time is ripe to start doubting as, indeed, many already do. Yet doubters come in different forms. Some respond by rejoicing in the fact that through popular access to global financial markets and their instruments, we can now escape the straitjacket of middle-class renunciations, outgrow expectations for security and piece-meal progress that would issue from our judicious consumption and incremental accretion of property and education, and instead get *A Piece of the Action*.[5]

Financial advice books encourage us to take the plunge, none with more spectacular success than Robert Kiyosaki's bestseller from the turn of the twenty-first century: *Rich Dad Poor Dad: What the Rich Teach Their Kids about Money—That*

5 J. Nocera, *A Piece of the Action: How the Middle Class Joined the Money Class* (New York: Simon and Schuster, 2013).

the Poor and Middle Class Do Not! Kiyosaki compares the advice he received from his two fathers. The first, a university professor, considered his home his largest asset and was always fretting about pay raises, retirement plans, medical benefits, sick leave, vacation days and other perks. He loved the university tenure system with its promise of steady employment. He wanted his son to study hard so that he could find a good company to work for. And he struggled financially all of his life and died leaving bills to be paid. The second was an entrepreneur who had barely finished the eighth grade but went on to become the richest man in Hawaii. He likened the person who would follow middle-class dad's advice to a cow ready for the milking. Rich dad recommended learning how money works, buying and selling assets frequently and with savvy, and always being on the lookout for new moneymaking opportunities. He is the undeclared hero whose voice is channeled in the book to wean readers from middle-class reticence and rouse them toward financial risks and fortunes.

Such books are evidently not written for a critical "we" but for the ambitious "I" who picks up on the failings of the middle-class ideology and wants to rise above the madding crowd that would continue producing all necessary goods and providing all necessary services. These books stand in stark contrast to a recent outpouring of literature whose authors and readers are less keen on gaming the system than they are on figuring out why the system fails and how it can be fixed. These texts diagnose a middle-class squeeze, especially but by no means exclusively in the US context, attributing it to such things as stagnant real-wage growth, diminished public support, job automation, the rising costs of health and education, the unrestrained power of speculative finance and corporate interests, vulnerability to financial crises, unjustified fees and inequitable tax burdens.[6] While critical of the predicaments they diagnose as plaguing the middle class, they rarely question the logic of the institutions that govern the lives of its purported members. Rather, they attribute these institutions' unfulfilled promises of security and prosperity to causes external to them. The reforms they propose are designed to make the usual middle-class investments in property, insurance and education pay off to the degree that they had in the past.

Anthropologists have one important advantage over purely conceptual theorists: the possibility of perceiving—through ethnographic research anchored in a broad understanding of what constitutes human experience and how it comes together—the interconnections between institutions that appear

---

6   For example, M. J. Casey, *The Unfair Trade: How Our Broken Global Financial System Destroys the Middle Class* (New York: Crown Publishing, 2012); D. Fergus, *Land of the Fee: Hidden Costs and the Decline of the American Middle Class* (Oxford University Press, 2016); S. T. Fitzgerald and T. L. Kevin, *Middle Class Meltdown in America: Causes, Consequences and Remedies*, second edition (London: Routledge, 2014); R. P. Formisano, *Plutocracy in America: How Increasing Inequality Destroys the Middle Class and Exploits the Poor* (Baltimore: Johns Hopkins University Press, 2015); R. H. Frank, *Falling Behind: How Rising Inequality Harms the Middle Class* (Berkeley: University of California Press, 2007); P. T. Hoffman, G. Postel-Vinay and J. L. Rosenthal, *Surviving Large Losses: Financial Crises, the Middle Class, and the Development of Capital Markets* (London: Harvard University Press, 2007); D. Madland, *Hollowed Out: Why the Economy Doesn't Work without a Strong Middle Class* (Berkeley: University of California Press, 2015); N. Mooney, *Not Keeping Up with Our Parents: The Decline of the Professional Middle Class* (Boston: Beacon, 2008); K. Phillips, *Boiling Point: Republicans, Democrats, and the Decline of Middle-Class Prosperity* (New York: Random House, 1993); K. Porter, *Broke: How Debt Bankrupts the Middle Class* (Stanford: Stanford University Press, 2012); T. A. Sullivan, E. Warren and J. L. Westbrook, *The Fragile Middle Class: Americans in Debt* (New Haven: Yale University Press, 2000).

to be separate, primarily between political, legal and economic ones, and those associated with culture, lifestyle and belief. This turns out to be of great value for the matter at hand because the ideology that summons the middle class into being manifests itself across the fault lines of economy, politics and culture. Anthropologists typically discuss middle classes in the plural to signal the heterogeneity of their alleged members. Drawing on extended fieldwork among these populations in a wide variety of countries and settings, they describe their social relations and subjective experiences in ways that convey the constraints to which they are subject. They pay particular attention to their patterns of work, consumption and political action. Then they trace how these patterns are interwoven with pressures and opportunities emerging out of national and global markets.[7]

I am greatly indebted to their insights and draw on them in

---

7   For example, D. Kalb, *Expanding Class: Power and Politics in Industrial Communities, The Netherlands, 1850–1950* (Durham: Duke University Press, 1997); W. Lem, "Articulating Class in Post-Fordist France," *American Ethnologist*, 2002, 29(2), 287–306; M. Lamont, *Money, Morals, and Manners: The Culture of the French and American Upper-Middle Class* (Chicago: University of Chicago Press, 1992); M. Liechty, *Suitably Modern: Making Middle-Class Culture in a New Consumer Society* (Princeton: Princeton University Press, 2003); M. Liechty, "Middle-Class Déjà Vu," in C. Freeman, R. Heiman and M. Liechty, eds., *The Global Middle Classes* (Santa Fe: SAR Press, 2012); J. Patico, *Consumption and Social Change in a Post-Soviet Middle Class* (Washington: Woodrow Wilson Center Press, 2008); Sumich, "The Uncertainty of Prosperity: Dependence and the Politics of Middle-Class Privilege in Maputo"; A. Truitt, "Banking on the Middle Class in Ho Chi Minh City," in M. Van Nguyen, D. Bélanger and L. B. Welch Drummond, eds., *The Reinvention of Distinction: Modernity and the Middle Class in Urban Vietnam* (New York: Springer, 2012); M. Saavala, *Middle-Class Moralities: Everyday Struggle over Belonging and Prestige in India* (New Delhi: Orient Blackswan, 2012); Maqsood, *The New Pakistani Middle Class*; and, for a wide

my analysis. I nevertheless approach the middle class from a different angle: that of immanent critique. Scholars have used immanent critique to various effects, their premise being that instead of criticizing a category or institution from the outside—which is at any rate impossible insofar as we actively partake in what we call into question—we can grasp it more fully by mining its inherent tensions and contradictions from within. To do so, we strategically take at face value the thing that we are interested in figuring out, and then follow the way it operates in the world or in people's lives in order to spot the places where its own logic falters. Anthropology has a penchant for immanent critique because of the field's emblematic methodology of ethnographic fieldwork. This method elicits the common ways in which things are defined and described, and triangulates them with interview data and with observation of people as they act over time and in specific settings within the institutions in question. This almost always brings

---

range of case studies, the contributions to the volumes edited by Freeman, Heiman and Liechty, *Charting an Anthropology of the Middle Classes*; by H. Li and L. L. Marsh, eds., *The Middle Class in Emerging Societies: Consumers, Lifestyles and Markets* (London: Routledge, 2016); and by H. Melber, ed., *The Rise of Africa's Middle Class: Myths, Realities, and Critical Engagements* (London: Zed Books, 2016). H. Donner, "The Anthropology of the Middle Class Across the Globe," *Anthropology of this Century*, 2017, 18, surveys this literature. See also L. Wacquant, "Making Class: The Middle Class(es) in Social Theory and Social Structure," in R. F. Levine, R. Fantasia and S. McNall, eds., *Bringing Class Back In* (Boulder: Westview Press, 1991), for an objection to defining and demarcating a middle class, and for a counterargument, D. Kalb, "Class," in D. M. Nonini, ed., *A Companion to Urban Anthropology* (New York: Blackwell, 2014), and D. Kalb, "Introduction: Class and the New Anthropological Holism," in J. G. Carrier and D. Kalb, eds., *Anthropologies of Class: Power, Practice and Inequality* (Cambridge: Cambridge University Press, 2015).

to the fore a host of tensions between the official and ideological logic of institutions, what people do in their framework, and the outcomes of their actions.

Such tensions are inevitable insofar as all categories and institutions have been designed at certain points in time to accomplish specific goals for particular groups of people. This holds true even when the most successful among them assume the appearance of universality and common sense, as though devoid of purpose or origin—a neutral and unquestioned thing. Such thing-ification (scholars sometimes call it essentialization or reification) of a historical contingency is the greatest power to which an ideology can aspire, making it appear beyond contestation, a fact of life. But the very idea is founded on impossibility. In a world populated by human beings who are distinct, complex and reflective, no particular objective can ever attain such a stronghold on everyone's thought and practice as to actually become as thing-like as it is sometimes held to be; hence the tensions and contradictions to be mined and deconstructed.

This is the approach I have taken in this book: I interrogate the category of middle class in its relation to capitalism in the first chapter, and then I proceed to relate it to institutions like private property in the second chapter and to human capital in the third, in order to expose their premises and promises. In the fourth chapter, I delineate features of politics and values commonly associated with the middle class. I tie the arguments together and follow some remaining threads in the conclusion. Throughout this inquiry, I bring examples from ethnographic studies that I have conducted in Israel and in Germany and from those that others have conducted elsewhere in the world. These explorations have triggered the revelations whose conclusions I formulate here. Even so, I spend the greater part of the book developing my arguments conceptually while using ethnographic data sparingly and for illustrative purposes alone. The literature on the lives and experiences of the people cast as global middle classes is already quite extensive and growing still. I reference some of the best of it in footnotes so that those interested in finding out more about the groups so designated can, in true middle-class spirit, make the necessary investments.

1
What We Talk about when We
Talk about the Middle Class

What do we talk about when we talk about the middle class? The critical half of the term is not "class" but "middle." It evokes a spectrum of gradated positions with people moving to and fro between lower and upper reaches. The middleness of middle class suggests space: we move socially and economically relative to people occupying higher or lower positions, inching closer to some and then to others. It also suggests movement in time: awareness that within the span of our own lifetimes we can ascend or descend. Consecutive generations of our families may do the same, impelling, continuing or altering our greater upward or downward trajectories. Our perpetual movement bespeaks restlessness. The middle class is sometimes spoken about as an aspirational group, drawn by prosperity within reach, and sometimes as an insecure one, haunted by a fear of falling. It is, as social critic Barbara Ehrenreich[1] put it, evanescent: requiring ever-renewed effort to assert and maintain one's social position.

---

1   B. Ehrenreich, *Fear of Falling: The Inner Life of the Middle Class* (New York: Pantheon Books, 1989).

In contrast to "middle," which is amplified in the way we talk about the middle class, "class" is toned down. In fact, class is muted to such an extent that, as some theorists have noted, saying "middle class" is almost like saying "no class at all."[2] They point out how middle classness summons neither a deeply held sense of identity (just compare it to things like race, religion, nationality, gender or sexual orientation), nor empathic allegiance to members of the same group, if a group is even acknowledged. One reason is that, unlike with slaves and masters, serfs and lords, or even, tellingly, workers and capitalists, there is no class to which the middle class stands in clear opposition. Instead, it replaces cohesive and demarcated groups with an image of multitudes of disconnected individuals. Each comes fully equipped with a personal history, drive and destiny, as if no fixed definition could possibly capture who they are, what they do and how they are likely to fare.

What is more, in recent decades we have come to perceive society as being comprised, quite simply, of middle classes and others. In this perception, "middle class" stands for normality: individuals who stand on their own two feet and progress or decline in a conventional way, which is to say systematically, independently and (barring exceptional occurrences) incrementally, without significant upheaval. This is seen as reflecting the standard nature of their investment and its rewards, or of their inertia and its penalties. Directly above the middle class, per public imagination, lounge elites who are spared the

---

2   L. Boltanski and E. Chiapello, *The New Spirit of Capitalism* (London: Verso, 2007); M. Savage, *Class Analysis and Social Transformation* (Philadelphia: Open University Press, 2000); S. Žižek, *The Ticklish Subject: The Absent Center of Political Ontology* (London: Verso, 2000).

effort of ascension and the danger of decline; while immediately below idle about the welfare-dependent underclasses and other marginal populations if our frame of reference is advanced economies, or destitute masses if we are looking further afield, all of whom appear, in contrast, to be shackled to their misery.

The idea of middle class as a class-neutral norm of individual self-determination is a denial of what "class" stands for. It negates the notion that indirect and impersonal forces might delimit our position in society or preordain the opportunities we will have and the quality of life we will enjoy. Class is stronger in indicating an external determination of our lives than categories like race, gender and religion. This is because social and economic opportunities are inherent in the concept of class (as opposed to, say, a member of a race or gender group being assigned a certain fate through the recognizable influence of place- and time-specific racism or sexism). To reject class or (what amounts to the same thing) to assert middle classness is to spurn the notion that our chances of success in life might be shaped by anything other than our own desires, capacities and, above all, efforts. And the middle class does this in a big way.

The potential to become middle class suggests that social mobility—both rising and falling—is our own doing. Finding the referent for "middle class" is tricky precisely because its boundaries are so fluid. Indeed, they have to be fluid for mobility to work. "Middle class" stands for open-ended meritocracy, holding forth a promise of entry to anyone who invests and the threat of decline over anyone who doesn't. Delaying gratification, sacrificing some consumption in order to put something aside, taking on the risk and commitment of indebted ownership and investing in education and training, in a home, in a savings plan, in a pension, are all middle-class strategies of rising and of taking precautions against falling. Middle classness implies that anyone can potentially ascend through effort, initiative and sacrifice, just as anyone can descend if they are fickle, lazy or wanting in aspiration. It pronounces us the masters of our destinies and kings of our fortunes. This applies just as forcibly to our image in the eyes of our peers: if we made it, we must have applied ourselves, and if we failed, we probably haven't and have no one to blame but ourselves.[3]

If this is what "middle class" means, what purpose does it serve? We might begin to answer this question by looking at its biggest fans, be they politicians or policy experts, corporations or marketing firms, development agencies or financial institutions: all those who intone moralizing proclamations about the middle class being harbingers of democracy, progress and consumption-fueled economic growth. They have markedly different and sometimes conflicting sensibilities and agendas when they seek the expansion of the middle class or speak up for middle-class interests and vulnerabilities. Common to all of them, however, is a de facto if rarely acknowledged attachment to capitalism, if only because they

---

3 Anthropologist Kathryn Dudley, having studied dispossessed farmers and unemployed autoworkers in the US, relays how, through material hardship, they continue believing that they are middle class in the sheer sense of being masters of their own destiny, despite the circumstances that have failed them. See: K. M. Dudley, *End of the Line: Lost Jobs, New Lives in Postindustrial America* (Chicago: University of Chicago Press, 1994); and K. M. Dudley, *Debt and Dispossession: Farm Loss in America's Heartland* (Chicago: University of Chicago Press, 2000).

depend on its workings for the accomplishment of their respective goals.

The most erudite apologia for so-called bourgeois virtues has been penned, tome after wordy tome, by economist Deirdre McCloskey, who finds in the middle class everything from honesty, through richer social, emotional and even spiritual lives, to motley identity choices.[4] Anyone who has ever visited an affluent community whose residents boast that they never lock their doors knows how annoying it is to have privilege name itself morality. But when someone as smart as McCloskey deems a manifold of virtues inextricable from the enormous privilege that is required to exercise them, she speaks in good capitalist faith. These gifts and sensibilities, she believes, are available to all of us as the spoils of economic growth: the more people out there who possess bourgeois virtues, the more whose lives will similarly be enriched as presumed billions already have been.

Literary critic Franco Moretti[5] reassigns as "middle class" what McCloskey calls "bourgeoisie," reminding us that by the nineteenth century it has come to replace the earlier, more rigid category because of its greater capacity to connote social mobility. With this in mind, we understand McCloskey to be saying that middle classes are capitalism's protagonists,

4 D. McCloskey, *The Bourgeois Virtues: Ethics for an Age of Commerce* (Chicago: University of Chicago Press, 2006); D. McCloskey, *The Bourgeois Era: Why Economics Can't Explain the Modern World* (Chicago: University of Chicago Press, 2010); and D. McCloskey, *Bourgeois Equality: How Ideas, Not Capital or Institutions, Enriched the World* (Chicago: University of Chicago Press, 2016).

5 F. Moretti, *The Bourgeois: Between History and Literature* (London: Verso, 2013).

actors whose virtues reflect those of capitalism itself, and whose proliferation marks the spread of its riches. Moretti goes on to observe how well the honesty that McCloskey attributes to members of the middle class aligns with the machinations of the capitalist market. An economic system's ideal typical actors need only play by the rules in order to enjoy its rewards: nothing is gained by trying to game so beneficent a system.

Proceeding from this insight, an obvious entry point to deciphering the category "middle class" lies in examining how capitalism works and the outcomes it promotes. Let me, then, briefly outline some aspects of capitalism that prefigure the purpose of the middle class within it.[6] McCloskey refuses to commit to a definition of capitalism beyond the trite notion of self-interested action that, let loose in healthy competition, encourages the gumption and enterprise that makes markets grow, with bountiful spillover effects—the famous rising tide lifting all boats. A more instructive starting point is one of capitalism's hallmarks: its foundation on a production process that, save few exceptions, is not centrally planned or coordinated. Unlike production in alternative or earlier social and economic systems, production in capitalism is not typically designed to generate the goods and services that would satisfy what people

---

6   In the following account of capitalism, I draw on K. Marx, *Capital, Vol 1.*, trans. B. Fowkes (London: Penguin, 1990); as well as on those among his commentators and updaters that I found most helpful, namely S. Clarke, *Marx's Theory of Crisis* (London: McMillan, 1994); D. Harvey, *Limits to Capital* (London: Verso, 2006); M. Heinrich, *An Introduction to the Three Volumes of Karl Marx's Capital*, trans. A. Locascio (New York: Monthly Review Press, 2004); and M. Postone, *Time, Labor, and Social Domination: A Reinterpretation of Marx's Critical Theory* (Cambridge: Cambridge University Press, 1993).

determine through democratic procedure or despotic decree to be needed by some or all of them. Instead, everyone is supposed to be free to produce what they will, and competition between producers decides the success or failure of each enterprise.

Proponents of capitalism like to say that this success or failure is ultimately a reflection of how well producers satisfy demand: no goods or services would ever be produced if people didn't want them enough to buy them. If they were, their producers would go out of business. Desire for goods and services signals to entrepreneurs that they could profit from their production, and these goods are consequently produced according to demand. Despite not being coordinated, then, popular needs and desires are ostensibly met through the free play of market mechanisms. What this line of reasoning elides is that even if popular demand, crucially backed by sufficient buying power, inscribes the ultimate boundaries for what any single enterprise can or cannot sell, it does so only after the fact of production. That is to say, after driving numerous entrepreneurs out of business, after permitting an overabundance of products to go to waste, and after leaving multiple needs unmet.

The crucial point is that these outcomes do not stem from producers' failure to accurately predict demand. Rather, they manifest the very logic of the capitalist system, which generates chronic overproduction. Producers, to avoid being priced out of business, need to outproduce and undersell their competitors. This competitive pressure is the motor that drives enterprise. Because of it, the things that end up being produced are not meant to satisfy needs or desires. Rather, they are designed to capture slices of the market through their amenability to cost cutting, their conduciveness to price raising, replacing and updating, and their capacity to induce demand for them through minute distinctions rendered personally meaningful. An ensuing excess of commodities—from groceries and entertainment through brands and fashions to a variety of professional services—competes for our wallets. Often, we either have no use for them or, far more commonly, we cannot afford to buy too many of them no matter how aggressively their manufacturers and retailers try to shove them down our throats.

As producers strive to attain a level of productivity that would give them a competitive edge over other producers, the entire production process changes. It incorporates innovative technology that speeds up and diversifies the provision of products, at the same time as it renders a lot of jobs redundant and squeezes as much work as possible out of every remaining employee. This accounts for capitalism's dynamism, thanks to which less and less overall work time is required to generate the economy's glut of commodities. It also accounts for the fact that, even as some people work so hard that they barely have time to see their loved ones, there are more people out there with the same skills who are suffering the effects of unemployment, underemployment and poverty. A hallmark of capitalism, when you consider it in its global totality, is the gross disparity between the mind-boggling amount of stuff that is produced and then left to waste, and at the same time the desperate deprivation and widespread struggle to earn basic necessities, or the backbreaking overwork by some alongside the demoralizing unemployment of others.

For the wheels of production to keep turning (and continue employing workers as well as financiers and auxiliary providers of machinery and services who would facilitate the production, circulation and sale of commodities), those who set these wheels in motion have to reinvest in their business to avoid losing it. But they also have to potentially profit from it to encourage the efforts and risks of multiple business endeavors. The economy must therefore have enough readily available and useable physical, material and financial resources to fuel enterprise and to incentivize the competition among various lines of business and industry. To guarantee this availability, there has to be incessant accumulation of a global surplus.

While an inanimate system cannot have a deliberate purpose, it can have a sort of inner dynamic that makes sense in terms of a goal it appears to be advancing. In capitalism, accumulation is this goal. Capitalism's cumulative excess is called surplus, because the capital that is accumulated globally cannot be invested profitably in the activities from which it stems, or be absorbed back into society in the form of anything the population could use or enjoy. A surplus is nevertheless always generated by overproduction, and the prospects of pocketing some of it as profit incentivizes entrepreneurial risk-taking. The goods and services that people can access and hold onto, in turn, must be limited in order to stimulate surplus-inducing competition among them for these things. Surplus's embodiment in profit or revenue, or in the expectation of profit or revenue sometime in the future, must likewise be high enough to urge reinvestment in ever more production of ever more commodities.

In a capitalist market, the general rule is for things to be exchanged freely for different things of equal value without force or theft. Under conditions of free and equivalent exchange, surplus can only be generated in one way: by workers producing more value in the form of the products and services to which their work contributes, than the value represented in the pay they receive for it. Karl Marx called this exploitation, because even when no one deliberately sets out to do anyone any harm and even when employers are just as happy or unhappy as their employees, work is not fully remunerated. The contribution in value that workers make to the commodities they help produce is larger than the value of the stuff they can purchase with their paychecks, however lowly or prestigious their jobs. And whatever they earn, even if they are earning good money, they are contributing to the production of more; otherwise no one would employ them and pay them for their work.

Additionally, earnings from work are generally (but with notorious exceptions) not enough to allow workers to ultimately stop working: otherwise there would not be enough workers to produce the economy's surplus. Finally, earnings from work should (again with exceptions) nevertheless suffice to finance workers' and their families' food and shelter, health, education and training at a level that is accepted in their society; otherwise the economy's workforce would not be up to the task of working and generating a surplus. Capitalism's accumulation through the extraction of unremunerated value from work and its embodiment as profit and revenue is made invisible when it is euphemized as growth. This gives surplus a positive aura of progress, deflecting attention from its human costs.

Competition between independent producers transforms the entire production process in a way that reduces barriers that might hamper or slow down the profitable production and circulation of goods and services. Small industry either grows to become large industry or disappears. Enterprise is economized through technological sophistication or else the entrepreneur is priced out of business. National economies are (unevenly) integrated into a world market in order to survive and—in the case of more powerful economies—to profit from business with less powerful ones. The subsequent increase in productivity makes it cheaper to produce all of the food, clothing, housing, transportation and other goods and services on which workers spend their paychecks. If they can buy the stuff they want for less money, employers and clients can pay workers less in aggregate and relative value. This, while their work and their services contribute more to the economy's surplus because they yield greater value than they cost. Capitalism thereby generates extraordinary wealth that is reinvested or concentrated at the top, however slowly or fitfully. It is a jagged trajectory whereby, despite advances and respites that workers in some regions or industries can win through political or personal victories, work loses value and employment conditions become more strenuous and precarious.

If surplus-extracting work was all that capitalism had to offer the people subject to it, however, it is hard to imagine how it could have remained intact for all this time, let alone gathered steam. Work could not always be hard and underpaid, with significant portions of the wealth that workers create escaping their reach, without these workers growing so disgruntled as to struggle constantly to break away or replace capitalism with a more just system of production and distribution. Historically, of course, workers have often tried to do just that. But others eschewed collective struggle, not only for threat of backlash but because they felt they had something to lose by revolting. A major factor entered the considerations of workers when they could finally, in large numbers, accrue a portion of the social surplus that they had themselves created.

It is hard to figure out anyone's precise contribution to goods and services whose composites are manufactured, combined and circulated by numerous people and machines, in multiple stages, separated from each other in time and space, and then to compare the value of these goods to the buying power represented in each worker's paycheck. Typically, we just assume that we're paid the competitive value of our work. We are certainly free—in theory at least, if seldom in practice—to charge a higher price for our services or seek employment elsewhere if we're unsatisfied. Sure, we might nevertheless recognize our collective disadvantage and organize to resist the system that disadvantages us. But when we are given something extra if we play by the rules—something whose existence and value are independent of our work, something the possession of which might give us leg up on those who do not possess it, and something the loss of which would be a calamity—we have good enough reason to turn a blind eye to our predicament.

When Marx wrote about class in his magnum opus *Capital*, he wrote about it in the structural sense, as the outcome of the production process being divided between ownership and non-ownership of the material resources it feeds on. He saw this division as generating antagonism between capital and labor: the less that labor is paid, the more resources can be accumulated in the form of a surplus that capital can pocket. And conversely, the greater the power of labor, the more of this surplus it can take back for itself. What Marx did not do in this study was to equate labor and capital with actual working classes and capitalist classes. Important reflections on the living conditions of workers and on aspects of class politics notwithstanding, his approach was more structural than historical, concerned with exposing the opaque logic of the capitalist system. But if we were to take a more historical approach, we would see that workers have indeed been enlisted into agendas associated with capitalists, in a way that has obscured the antagonism between labor and capital that Marx described. This, if you will, is the true purpose of the middle class.

We can have some of the surplus we create and enjoy it, too, despite our vulnerability as people who have to work for a living and despite the exploitation of our work in the creation of surplus. The institution that affords us this benefit is the very institution that has deprived us of the means to secure our livelihoods independently: private property. If we live in a capitalist society, we have no choice but to work under the conditions we are offered. These conditions are exploitative in the sense that our work generates a surplus we do not enjoy. We no longer live off of communal lands or obtain our basic necessities from other common resources. Working for less than the value of our work is therefore the only way for us to earn the money with which we can buy the things we need and want.

From around the seventeenth century onward, shared and common resources have been expropriated and parceled out, most often by force and against immense resistance, in the form of private property, that is, land and other resources that only some people got to own and control. The process was gradual in Europe and then more abrupt in colonial takeovers of other parts of the world. The beginnings of capitalism and its global spread came hand in hand with the violent introduction of private property where it had previously been absent or marginal to the ways in which populations managed their resources. As resources worldwide came to be parceled out in this way, people were left with no choice but to work for a living in whatever conditions the new owners of land, raw material, work instruments and other resources offered them.

There is another way of looking at property, however, which is promulgated by the agents and agencies of capitalism. This approach builds on the legal apparatus that designates and protects everyone's right to private ownership. The domain of ownership expands to encompass all manner of things that workers and their families covet: material things like a home or a car, immaterial assets like a savings account, an insurance policy, a pension contract, or a range of stock, bonds and securities—and to broaden the scope even further, other things like a university degree, a specialized skill, a professional credential or a social network, which usually fall under the heading of human capital.

We have a pretty good intuitive sense of what the possession of such things can do for us. The value that private property represents is independent of the value we earn by working. In the case of human capital, it could help us attain a better job. Our fortunes as workers can be counterbalanced by our fortunes as property owners. This matters whenever they diverge significantly. We might lose our earnings following employment cutbacks, falling demand for our services, health or family issues, or simply old age. Faced with such difficulties, owning a home, a savings account, an insurance policy or a university degree can mitigate the loss by securing new income. Alternatively, we might have purchased real estate, stock, or professional credentials, which market developments could make more valuable than when we procured them. This property can then help us cash in on a sum greater than what our work earnings alone would have brought in.

As workers who are at the same time existing or aspiring property owners, we do not assess our place in society (or the society that so places us) solely by the nature of our work and its pay. Nor do we see our collective predicament, as workers, as the be-all and end-all of our highly differentiated fortunes. Instead, all of the things we privately own or have the prospect of someday owning tug at our attention. As workers, we may be fully aware that the lower our paychecks in aggregate, the more the agents and agencies representing capital gain at our expense. But as property owners we stand in a more complicated relation to capitalist institutions. Often, we sense that to be able to leverage our possessions in order to secure our future or to improve our prospects by acquiring new property, we have to root for the stability and growth of our national economy. This holds particularly true when this growth is connected to the increase in the value of the property and assets we own, even if this growth is ultimately based on surplus accumulated at the expense of our wages. With the internalization of this sensibility, accumulation has us on board.

There is more to this shift in perspective than just learning to love capitalism. As people who have to work for a living, we crave property more the less reliable and rewarding our earnings from work and our other protections might be. But getting our hands on property, unless we are lucky enough to have inherited it, takes effort and sacrifice. We have to work harder and better than we otherwise would—perhaps harder and better than others do—if we want to earn enough to put something aside. Earmarking some of our earnings for a savings account, a university degree, a house or a pension, means that we cannot spend all of our earnings on the stuff we want right now. Even if we do attain some property immediately on credit or through installment plans, those debts have to be paid off sometime. Ultimately, then, we still have to work harder and save more. We have a word for our pursuit of property: investment. We invest more time, effort and resources than we absolutely must, in order to later have a potential income that does not rely on our work. We perceive this as a means by which to protect ourselves against a possible shortfall in our earnings and by which to spare ourselves or our children the need to work as hard in the future.

The growing popularity of the category "middle class" over the late nineteenth century in Europe's most advanced economies had everything to do with the proliferation of diverse forms of household property and of the means of obtaining it. This was also a time of social and political upheaval, which endangered the mounting force and dominance of capitalism. Operating to smooth the course of accumulation by appeasing disgruntled workforces, some of the surplus generated by the increased volume of industry became accessible to the populace. It was condensed into resources that allowed significant numbers of workers to become socially mobile and materially protected in ways they hadn't before. This mobility and protection, or the promise thereof, redirected their energies from protest to investment. Discontented workers could accrue savings, homes or credentials they would be terrified to lose. They could also acquire a broad array of material and cultural accoutrements through which to assert their advantages and showcase their accomplishments.

The benefit for accumulation lay in the creation of a docile and motivated workforce whose members are too busy trying to keep up in the scramble for property and property-dependent income to recognize and resist their common exploitation. Observing this trend, some theorists have written about the middle class as occupying a contradictory position between work and capital.[7] Contradictory, in the sense of pitting us against ourselves: as workers, we are exploited for the creation of surplus no matter how prestigious our jobs or how high our earnings. Yet, insofar as we own or have the hopes of procuring some savings, a home, a car, an insurance policy or a credential, we have something to gain by siding with the cumulative dynamic of capital, which might protect or increase the value of what we own, no matter how humble our jobs or how modest our earnings. We also have something to lose by resisting it insofar as our well-being hinges on the continued possession and preserved value of what resources we have managed to acquire.

We are classified in a way that applauds our propensity to look beyond the tight limitations on our work toward a future in which our households will soar or tumble as a result of our investments today, and to disregard the institutional constraints that, to sustain profitability, determine the value of our possessions, work and earnings, and by extension our own fates. We are named middle class. This designation opens its arms to all of us, from the highest-earning professionals and managers, through successful or struggling business owners

7 G. Carchedi, "On the Economic Identification of the New Middle Class," *Economy and Society*, 1975, 4(1); E. O. Wright, *Classes* (London: Verso, 1985).

and self-employed service providers, to the lowliest personnel and precariously employed interns. This is the case insofar as we make most of our living off work yet possess, or have the prospect of someday possessing, material and human resources whose value can be maintained or enhanced through investment. The designation "middle class" represents our consideration of what we own and how we fare as if they were the outcomes of our personal choices and efforts. It further represents our commitment to sacrificing for our future as if this future relied on our choices and efforts alone.

What makes this idea so compelling is that, to the extent that the value of our possessions does not change too radically while also making us better off than people who own less, or better protected against misfortune than we would have been without them, our best efforts often do pay off. We can therefore plausibly consider our pains to acquire property as prudent investments rather than compulsory forfeitures or reckless gambles. The more strenuously we work and study, plot careers and save for a home, for old age or for our children's education, the more engrossed we become in these endeavors and the greater our inclination to trace our fortunes back to them, above all else. Moreover, the more we delay gratification in anticipation of something better, the more reluctant we become to discredit our renunciations as externally imposed and therefore personally meaningless. We not only invest but also take pride in our investments and in ourselves for having made them.

But wait. What if we find we have had quite enough of struggling, competing and investing? What if, at some point, we decide that whatever assets we have already managed to ferret away give us a fair shot at living the kind of life we want to live, and that it is high time to sit back and reap what we have sown? Economists call the incomes generated by property "rents" and those who live off them "rentiers." They distinguish rents from the earnings that come from work and from the profits that come from enterprise. The fantasy of rentier leisure is one in which we can afford to work less, selectively or not at all, by living off our property. This sounds great for us but not so much for capitalism's imperative of accumulation. The institution of private property can very well boomerang for capitalism in the sense of providing not a common incentive but a common disincentive to work and invest.

And there's more. With only so much surplus generated through each cycle of production, how thinly—from the standpoint of potential profitability—can it be spread in globally available household property on top of other hoards of cash or assets that working households can simply hold on to for a rainy day? Recall that the promise of profit appropriated from the economy's surplus has the potential to encourage production's independent organizers, facilitators and financiers to forge ahead, risks and all. When a broad spectrum of the population has the political power to reclaim a portion of the surplus in the form of privately stored savings, cars, homes, social protections, academic degrees and the like, this could prove too heavy a drag on profitability and growth, even if most of them still work for a living. Economists have been discussing such dangers since household property has become pervasive, and tinkering with solutions that chip away at it, such as inflation and taxation. But the most insidious solution has been taking shape in recent decades, following an era of unprecedented growth in the rates of property ownership and the proliferation of household assets and savings.

Over the course of the 1980s and 1990s, national and regional markets have been deregulated and integrated into a global financial market, easing the flow of capital and the provisioning of credit to governments and firms everywhere in the world. It has helped stimulate competition and make accumulation smoother and more flexible. Capital is fed to profitable enterprises while overcoming social and geographic barriers between them. It is also withheld from enterprises that do not perform as well, regardless of their significance for national economies and regional populations. Novel financial instruments allow the risks attached to different kinds of investment (like changes in currency values or interest rates) to be pooled, subdivided, priced and sold off as further investment products. As a result, the volume of trade and enterprise as well as the bulk of global investment capital has grown exponentially, all the while creating new risks and opportunities for profit. Economic actors facing intensified competition as well as pressures by shareholders to increase the value of their holdings have come to rely on financing to survive and prosper. The reliance cuts both ways, as the intensification of economic activity and competition has amplified pressure on the global financial market to provide credit, bonds and shares, channel investment and manage risk.

The profit-hungry agencies of global finance are ever on the prowl for new investment opportunities, including in goods and services that had previously been financed publicly through taxes and social insurance arrangements, or privately through work earnings and bank-deposited savings. Industrial capitalism has given way to finance capitalism, flagging the dominance of global finance in public and private funding arrangements and in setting the terms for economic growth.

Risk estimates and pricing signal, to investors, avenues of potential profit or loss. Through this pricing, finance comes to regulate all aspects of economic, political and social life. It insinuates itself into the way in which institutions operate, the infrastructure through which services are provided, and the choices that national economies as well as firms and enterprises must weigh in order to remain viable.

The scholarly term for finance's dominance in the economy and society is "financialization." In advanced economies, financialization has dovetailed with other economic trends grouped under the heading of neoliberalism, mainly the decreased readiness of states to pool risks, stabilize incomes and provide goods and services through taxation and social insurance arrangements. The public safety nets that had spread piecemeal after the Second World War in advanced economies have been rolled back to varying degrees in each of them. Salaries have not grown apace with rising prices, while employment has become more precarious with the removal of work protections and the weakening of organized labor. The convergence of stagnant and unreliable work incomes with diminishing public goods and services has created urgent need among workers and citizens to counter mounting insecurity with whatever resources they manage to get their hands on.

Enter global finance. Through credit cards, installment plans, mortgages, student loans and other long-term lending, along with the financial management of savings, insurances and pensions, financial institutions rush in to cater to cultivated mass demand; hence the growing significance of financial services and instruments in household economics. This is accompanied by an imperative that requires anyone ensnared in the web of finance to become financially literate, able to recognize investment opportunities and use financial instruments with discernment while shouldering risks and taking responsibility for the outcomes of their investments or lack thereof. This responsibility often includes a self-imposed reduction in spending to balance family budgets and make sure that one's capital inflows and outflows are sustainable over time.

To ease the ongoing circulation of capital, institutional investors such as banks, insurance companies and pension funds intermediate between households and global finance. They do so through the provisioning and management of mortgages, pensions and other long-term savings products, insurance policies and consumer credit. They bundle the payments and repayments organized by these products, and they price them in bulk before selling them on to other market players. The value that household property represents flows back into the market to become credit for more investment. Because the value of this property is implicated in the ebb and flow of financial markets, it is itself in flux. Consider all those homes whose value is finally determined only after thirty years of mortgage repayments whose size changes, in turn, according to interest rates and currency values. Consider also retirement annuities determined by savings invested over decades in potentially volatile stocks and bonds. Then consider academic degrees whose price is calculated over many years of student-loan repayments while relying for validation on a mercurial job market. The danger of property providing too much security, or of its taking too much away from the economy's surplus, is lifted by the proliferation, among high and low earners alike, of property of unstable value. This kind of property requires invigorated investment while delivering erratic returns. All but the wealthiest owners cannot dream of finally settling for what assets they've succeeded in piecing together. Instead, many more are lured in by the promise of ownership, only to discover that in order to enjoy its benefits they must continue to relentlessly invest.

From our perspective, finance can help us buy the stuff that our earnings from work are too low for us to afford. It sounds great until we realize that household debt and low earnings go hand in hand. The more accustomed we become to buying things with credit cards, mortgage contracts and installment plans—which is bound to happen when they are too expensive for us to afford otherwise—the less our employers can get away with paying us. This is one sense in which financialization ratchets up our exploitation. Another is by disadvantaging us as investors who rely on assets like homes and pensions, which are relatively rigid and undiversified, in an investing climate that favors speed and flexibility. Yet another is by intensifying competition between industries, businesses and service branches, many of which respond by initiating cutbacks and layoffs and squeezing more value out of the workers they employ. Another still is by rendering exploitation so abstract—a pressure to which workers as well as capitalists are subject, imposed by an impersonal market and justified by the necessity to provide value for multiple, unidentified shareholders—that we cannot even blame our employers for paying us too little.[8]

8 D. Bryan and M. Rafferty, *Capitalism with Derivatives: A Political Economy of Financial Derivatives, Capital and Class* (New York: Palgrave MacMillan, 2006); D. Bryan and M. Rafferty, "Reframing Austerity:

But the final turn of the screw is that financialization makes us invest in our own exploitation. Banks and other financial market players bundle and repackage our payment and debt-repayment streams to sell them off as investment products to corporate entities and institutional investors. These investors are all too happy to pay now for income streams projected onto the future, in hopes that they will produce sums of greater value than their purchase price. The price of these financial products is calculated according to estimates of the risk that future repayments will cease or fall short: the higher the risk, the cheaper the products. Financial investors of all kinds protect themselves against this risk by compiling many unrelated financial products in a diversified portfolio. The diversified portfolio is itself priced in a way that takes into account events that might slow down or terminate the sources of its composite revenue streams: things like political unrest, a social uprising or widespread inability of debtors to service their loans. The pricing of assembled investment products thereby signals to governments and firms that they had better keep their citizens, workers and debtors in check to avoid divestment and loss.

Whether or not we are aware of it, we buy these products all the time through our pension and other long-term savings products. Our institutional investors choose these products for us to assure the viability of our pension claims or to maximize the value of our savings plans and other assets, as well as for their own profit. The same instruments we rely on in order to save up for homes and higher education or to provision for old

---

Financial Morality, Saving and Securitization," *Journal of Cultural Economy*, 2017, 10(4), 339–55; B. Lee and E. LiPuma, *Financial Derivatives and the Globalization of Risk* (Durham: Duke University Press, 2004).

age are instruments designed to support the accumulation of surplus at whatever cost to society. By prudently and conscientiously investing in the well-being of our families, we are also investing in a system that dominates us by managing our work and resources in a way that chips away at our powers as workers and citizens. This creates what some critics of financialization call its cannibalistic features, generalizing the exploitation of each over all.[9]

Just as the value of our own money cannot be divorced from the circulation of capital, so can we not assess our precise role in the process of accumulation. The degradation of our work and exacerbation of our insecurity proceed in ways that we can seldom trace back to our disadvantaged encounters with capital, particularly when our own assets are thrown into the mix. What does strike us in our everyday experiences is the easy access we have to financing. Consider all those credit card applications clogging our mailboxes, the loans we are offered left and right, the potentially inflation-outstripping investments that our savings are directed toward, and the expensive commodities we are invited to acquire now while paying for them bit by bit. It feels like we are being enfranchised and empowered as earners, savers, owners and investors. Those of us with the wherewithal to invest use financial instruments to procure precautionary and aspirational assets like a home, a pension and a university degree. To the extent that we can, we

---

9   R. Martin, *The Financialization of Daily Life* (Philadelphia: Temple University Press, 2012); S. Soederberg, "Cannibalistic Capitalism: The Paradoxes of Neoliberal Pension Securitization," *Socialist Register*, 2010, 47; D. Sotiropoulos, J. Milios and S. Lapatsioras, *A Political Economy of Contemporary Capitalism and Its Crisis: Demystifying Finance* (New York: Routledge, 2013).

undertake the long-term planning required of us as borrowers, savers and family members. Accomplishing all that, we can overlook the conditions of our work and citizenship while adopting the perspective that these assets stand for. We can see ourselves as taking charge of our lives through self-reliant investment, prudent saving, personal responsibility and long-term strategizing. We can see ourselves as middle class.

Our erratic movement through the range of investment opportunities pulls us ever more deeply into the chase. When rewards appear forthcoming but are also hard to come by, we exert ourselves in hunting them down and are not discouraged from trying harder when we fail. Credit has that kind of effect on our relation to property and investment: placing all of the things that our dreams are made of at the tip of our fingers, while forcing us to work harder and reach deeper into our pockets to grasp and hold on to them. It also motivates us to keep working and reaching when the things we procure turn out not to have the value we were counting on. As we keep giving while capital keeps accumulating behind our backs and at our expense, we bite our lips and soldier on because that is what perceiving ourselves as middle class inspires us to do.

The middle-class sense of self-determination is even more striking where finance has been making inroads into the "emerging" or "developing" economies (as they are often called) of Asia, Africa and Latin America. These economies have been undergoing liberalization in the sense of opening up to international trade and investment as well as to an influx of commodities and the financial instruments with which to attain them. Most of the population in these places had in previous decades squeaked by, often modestly or miserably, with very few private possessions. Suddenly, many among them are receiving loans to buy things that used to be unattainable. Consequently, the price of health care, education, housing and transportation in these places has been skyrocketing. It buries those whose lifestyles direct them to use the more efficient of these services under the usual mountain of debt. They have to strategize, manage risks, redouble workloads and seek new sources of income in order to service this debt. In most cases, they do so in the absence of adequate work and protections. The newly minted investors of emerging economies—now christened the rising global middle classes—are handed the reins of their futures. But they quickly discover that these reins are entangled with the economic, social and emotional tolls of the financialized property.

It turns out that there is nothing contradictory after all in the talk of a squeezed middle class in one part of the world and a rising middle class in another. The global financial market now grows by tinkering with asset values in rich countries as well as by investing in new assets in poor ones. Where people already have a few decades' worth of accumulated private property, public resources and human capital, they are suddenly discovering that these assets and protections come at a higher price or that their value is unreliable, and they feel the pinch in their pocketbooks. And where people have previously owned next to nothing, but a world of property and the means to finance it suddenly opens up to them, they are newly enlisted as aspirational investors. The designation of "middle class" is malleable enough to include these new entrants in a domain where greater luxury has been the general rule.

Economist Branko Milanovic calls them the respective losers and winners of global finance, lamenting that growing global income is unequally apportioned.[10] Yet, inequalities in distribution notwithstanding, the more dramatic growth is not of income earmarked for anyone's use, but of surplus. And surplus can only provisionally benefit those who are in a position to pocket some of it in the form of rent or revenue while subjecting them, and everyone else who works for a living, to exploitation and its attendant evils.

Being middle class means being good troopers and overlooking the big picture. The people most likely to do so are workers with the means to attain some property, who live in societies in which this property can make a difference to their lives. With the backwind of a middle-class ideology, they invest more time, work or resources than they otherwise would, and more than they are immediately rewarded for, with their future in mind. Since this attitude is so useful for accumulation, the people who rely on the institutions of capitalism for their jobs and positions deplore what they consider the middle-class squeeze, seeking ways to reenergize longtime investors who languish under the burden of erratic and unremunerated investments. They also celebrate the rise of a global middle class, taking heart from untold millions that they represent as willing investors in, rather than hapless victims of, the ascent to dominance of finance capitalism.

With all of the advantages that financialization offers to the cause of capitalist accumulation, it also lays bare some of accumulation's fault lines. The image of self-accomplished social mobility relies on a notion of investment: that the property we sacrifice for now will afford us returns we can

---

10   B. Milanovic, *Global Inequality: A New Approach for the Age of Globalization* (Cambridge, MA: Harvard University Press, 2016).

count on in the future. That is why when we put some of our earnings aside as savings or installments in durable purchases rather than spending them all on consumer goods, we do not see ourselves as foolhardy speculators but as prudent and responsible workers, citizens and family members. Anthropologist David Graeber captures the spirit of investment when he writes that being middle class means feeling that the fundamental social institutions exist for our benefit, that if we play by the rules we can predict results, and that we can plot even our children's futures assuming that the rules will stay the same.[11] But he misses the mark when he sees this feeling wavering as we are weighed down by debt. Debt on its own is not the problem. It undeniably weighs us down, yet we continue to take out loans to protect against falling or to reach upward with even greater aplomb. The availability of credit is many workers' only shot at better futures. The propensity of people from patently low ranks of society to consider themselves middle class is evidence of this ideology's tenacity against hardship and struggle, a tenacity often fortified directly through precautionary and aspirational indebtedness. It is capitalism itself, rather than the financial instruments (like credit and debt) it wields, that dooms our struggles. This, insofar as we continue being exploited, locked in competition and prey to dynamics beyond our control, which validate or devalue whatever investments we make.

The real turning point in our potential awareness comes when the value of our indebted property becomes too unpredictable to make the promises prefigured by investment in it

---

11   D. Graeber, "Anthropology and the Rise of the Professional-Managerial Class," *HAU: Journal of Ethnographic Theory*, 2014, 4(3), 73–88.

plausible. This does not mean that we are less enamored of the notion of being middle class or less prone to investing in the property and human capital associated with it. But it does allow us to see more clearly, if we look hard enough, the predicaments that this aggravates. No ideology is airtight: it takes a certain constellation of material and social conditions to make it convincing. An ideology that relies so heavily on the idea of investment needs investment to retain its charms. The growing availability of household property has allowed capitalism to fashion people's identities as investors rather than workers. Financialized access to property has inspired more and more people all over the world to self-identify in this way. In advanced economies, social policy and regulation have succeeded, in the decades after the Second World War, in providing projected returns to investing citizens. So long as workers' investments have been rewarded in expected ways, they have also been self-validating. So much so that they have drawn workers' attention away from the creeping, behind-the-scenes devaluation of their work, even as this work remained the primary means by which they financed their daily living.

With financialization reshaping societies worldwide, things are starting to change. The risks that bedevil household balance sheets and the irregularity of returns on investments form the cracks through which we can potentially see, beyond our protections and preconceptions, that the game itself is rigged. Contrary to its own rhetoric, our economic system is not made up of our self-advancing yet mutually beneficial choices and efforts, but of the imperative to feed accumulation by always giving more than what we get. From the perspective of what we must exert nowadays for the sake of our security and well-being and the likely outcomes of our exertions, we can look back and discover that we have always been played. Our efforts and investment have, since the dawn of capitalism, been mobilized and exploited toward the accumulation of surplus. The only difference is that now, the crumbs scattered in our direction are smaller and more intermittent. This difference might open our eyes to the reality that for all of the upbeat pull-yourself-up-by-the-bootstraps rhetoric middle classness generates, we are not, and have never been, middle class.

2

The Discreet Charm of Property

One thing that the recent financial crisis has made brutally clear is that property is not to be trusted. Despite having played by the rules, millions of people have been priced out of their homes. Others have lost purportedly safe retirement plans as well as long-term savings and investments. Still others carry massive burdens of student debt for degrees that have no pull in the job market. You would think that after such an upheaval we would all be rather leery about squirreling away our hard-earned money in what has become more of a gamble than a sure thing. Not so: property markets are booming. Many people continue to stretch their resources thin, sometimes along with those of their parents and other benefactors, and they take on all of the risks and obligations of long-term debt, only to acquire assets of questionable value.

In Luis Buñuel's 1972 surrealist film, *The Discreet Charm of the Bourgeoisie*, the characters' attempts at fine dining are thwarted time and again, yet they doggedly keep trying. Stranded, finally, on a desolate road to nowhere, they march onward with a show of self-assurance. We, too, are tenacious in our middle-class pursuits despite the frustrations they entail. There's a compulsive feel to our resolve with respect to property. Acquiring it seems like a necessary step in our quest for security, at the very least—or prosperity, should we set our sights higher. We have it pegged as an investment, if not necessarily the best or even a good one. As an investment, property constitutes a benchmark for responsible and forward-looking adulthood, in part to offset the insufficiency or undesirability of alternative support from jobs, government and relatives. If not in homes, pensions, insurance policies, savings accounts, financial assets, academic degrees and professional qualifications, in what are we to invest?

I puzzle in this chapter through the mystery of our nervous pursuit of property in order to show the way it reflects the contradictions inherent in the middle class. My argument is that the allure of property emboldens us to invest more and better than we otherwise might, just as conceived by a dominant vein of liberal thought. We invest in property for the security it represents in a competitive environment where ownership yields interpersonal advantage. Yet, through the vehicle of property, our money flows to a market whose growth destabilizes the conditions that might help us achieve the security we seek. The unreliable value of financialized property forces us to keep investing nonetheless in order to prop it up. Investment in property proceeds differently, however, according to the social and political arrangements that regulate property values and pursuits, which I will elaborate on later in this chapter.

But first: a case study. I have been wondering for some time about the preponderance of investment in property whose value is unreliable, but it took me a while to find an ethno-graphic means of exploring it. The problem is that, normally, we accumulate property over our entire lifetime, investing in academic credentials here, buying a home on mortgage there, deducting portions of our earnings for pensions, savings and insurance policies, without stepping back to take stock of our accrued property and its total value. This is to the advantage of an accumulation process that feeds on our investments: we are more likely to invest in the usual things when we have no clear notion of what we gain or lose by it. But there is an exception to this rule: divorce. When people divorce, they have to divvy up their marital property, including the kind that is not physically divisible, like a home or an insurance policy. This division occurs in the throes of the economic set-back that divorce brings about, when the value of one's belongings seems critical. I set about studying divorces in Israel, then, to gain a better understanding of what property means for its owners.

The idea of property as investment incarnate is one of those enduring legacies of seventeenth-century liberalism that lives on in divorce law today, in Israel as in most liberal democracies. A dominant strand of economic liberal thought proposes that people are likely to invest more when they believe in imminent returns. It makes no difference, from this perspective, what form the property they invest in takes or what it means to those who own it. Private property is simply an incentive for all members of society to apply themselves for the prospect of future returns, generating thereby the productivity that makes the economy grow. It supports another strand of liberal thought that considers the fruits of economic growth to be available to all those contributing to it in proportion to their inputs. These strands intertwine to form the common belief that private property, as the organizing principle of society's resources, makes us collectively wealthier.

Modern divorce law operates in the shadow of this belief, determining household property to be the fruit of marital investments and concluding divorces by its division. Legal process aims to bring about an equal division of marital property, even if it is not physically divisible or if only one spouse officially owns it. This is thought to reflect the different yet equal investments of divorcing spouses in their joint household, for example when one was a breadwinner and the other a homemaker. Most divorcees I spoke with tried to settle their divorces out of court. The legal injunction to divide property equally served them as a reference point, but more often than not, they came up with creative ways of dividing their property unequally or leaving it intact. When I asked them about their respective investments in the marital property, most brushed the idea off: they sought solutions that would allow each of them to land on their feet and get on with their lives.

One woman was emerging from a thirteen-year marriage. During the marriage she had put her career as a therapist on hold to bring up her children, so her income remained small. Her husband's income was not much higher; he was a doctoral student in the humanities and a translator on the side. They were barely making ends meet when married, and divorce pushed them to the brink. They partly owned their home thanks to her parents' help with the down payment, but they were still making mortgage payments. Neither of them could afford to buy out the other's share or to pay the mortgage alone. So they sold the home and gave her most of its value to buy a smaller apartment instead. A split down the middle would have left neither with enough to buy a new home and they wanted one for the children. They also agreed that he would pay less child support than the law specifies but the most he could afford while pursuing a PhD. He promised to increase the sum upon attaining a university position. Just as he had started making the payments, his publisher went under. Her parents took over the child-support payments while he went looking for a new part-time job.

This is but one example of a more ambivalent attitude to property among many I witnessed. They included a couple taking out a joint mortgage to keep their second home and using it to finance the rent of the husband who had moved out; a woman forfeiting her share of her ex-husband's stocks in return for the family home; a man taking upon himself the entire marital debt in return for keeping his retirement savings for himself; a woman buying off her ex-husband's half of the house by discounting the sum from his monthly child-support payments; and a couple putting the house under the children's names. I have also seen divorcees cutting back on expenses, forgoing promising careers for more secure employment, soliciting money, residence or childcare from their parents, cashing in on social security and fighting tooth and nail over child support. Property was not their primary fallback, nor did they assess it with reference to past investments or future value. They cared far less about ownership than they did about how to use what they had to stabilize their families' economic situation. In dire straits, property revealed its true colors. Shining through my study was not preoccupation with its nature, value and judicious division. Common concern was rather over what anthropologists studying so-called middle classes worldwide called a longing to secure.[1]

The calamity of divorce notwithstanding, there is no denying that this longing is often expressed precisely through the vehicle of private property. In the previous chapter I referenced an affinity between the middle class and property. It is historical affinity: the designation "middle class" having gained traction alongside the spread of property of the relatively expensive and durable kind, which families could purchase and own. The affinity is also conceptual, with both notions issuing from the idea that material fortunes are the outcome of personal investment. Middle-class identification is most credible among workers who invest some of their earnings or borrow resources for the sake of future goals, instead of spending them all on current desires. Property is a vehicle that channels these investments and promises to store their value for the future. I also mentioned how useful it is for capitalism to have some of the economy's accumulated surplus diverted into assets that absorb workers' attention as property owners. This distracts them from their collective exploitation and encourages them to work harder, seek credit and pour their earnings back into circulation.

The sway of property is real enough, seeing as it often delivers on its investment potential by affording owners interpersonal and temporary advantages. Those who own property are by and large better off materially than those who don't and better off than they might themselves have been had they not invested in it. Yet this is by no means always the case, as the

---

1   C. Freeman, R. Heiman and M. Liechty, eds., *Charting an Anthropology of the Middle Classes* (Santa Fe: SAR Press, 2012), 20.

prevalence of property booms and busts, unexpected side costs and supplementary expenses perennially remind us. And even when true, property's advantages are only relative to those of others and are therefore provisional and tenuous. Most importantly, property, for those who do not own a great deal of it, seldom provides the security or prosperity it foreshadows. Making it a stand-in for security is therefore nothing but an ideology. And much like the ideology of the middle class, it triggers action that does not necessarily accomplish the goals prefigured by it.

A recent analysis of the financial lives of 235 households in the United States shows this clearly.[2] In the course of the year in which they have been studied, these families experienced unsteadiness in both incomes and expenses, with sudden unexpected spikes and dips. This turbulence elevated the potential significance of their property in weathering it. Yet the property they owned or pursued exacerbated their predicaments as much as it allayed them. Typical in this respect were the Johnsons, defined by the analysts as a middle-class family according to income levels and accoutrements. Both husband and wife earned steady incomes from work yet their expenses were unpredictable. These expenses included large sums they had to pay for car repair, home repair and health care crises as well as Christmas and birthday gifts for their children. Rather than budgeting to prioritize short-term necessities like paying bills on time, they placed their bets on property-dependent upward mobility. The wife enrolled in college in the hopes that an academic degree would help her secure a higher paying job. It

---

2   J. Morduch and R. Schneider, *The Financial Diaries: How Americans Cope in a World of Uncertainty* (Princeton: Princeton University Press, 2017).

was by no means clear that it would, plus (she joked) she would be forty by the time she graduated and paying off the college loan for the rest of her life. Also, she and her husband bought a house, hoping that it would constitute a reserve for the future. But the mortgage payments were a heavy burden, while repair costs kept biting into their budgets. Making things worse, the value of the house remained stagnant. The Johnsons, meanwhile, dealt with constant stress.

The origins of unrelenting investment in property dovetail with those of the middle class. The rapid economic growth that followed the industrial revolution in parts of Europe made a range of new professional, service and managerial positions spring up, paying more than the agricultural or factory work of the time. New moneymaking opportunities also emerged, expanding the material diversity and social gradation of the populations among which capitalism was most advanced. But the greater variety of occupations and fortunes did not mean that the people who began working in different jobs or earning more money also played different roles in their society or attained distinct status. Historian Dror Wahrman tells how, despite the social and economic diversity in nineteenth-century England, there was no burgeoning social group that "middle class" could demarcate.[3] Yet this did not stop politicians from invoking the designation as a rhetorical device. They promoted their agendas by proclaiming the middle class to be key actors in realizing whatever political and economic reforms they proposed and the ones most likely to benefit

---

3   D. Wahrman, *Imagining the Middle Class: The Political Representation of Class in Britain 1780–1840* (Cambridge: Cambridge University Press, 1995).

from their implementation. Political consent could be secured by shifting the responsibility for well-being to citizens' own investments and by drawing out a horizon in which these investments bear fruit.

The chief advantage of this designation was in facilitating accumulation by arming the workers best positioned to contribute to it with aspiration, industriousness and enterprise. In his magisterial history of the rise and consolidation of modern capitalism, Eric Hobsbawm lingered on the new social climbers whose self-betterment was related to the changing nature of property.[4] Aristocratic landlords and estate owners topped the traditional hierarchies of old. By the nineteenth century, estates gave way, albeit partly and unevenly, to more modest forms of property that people without prior endowments of land and capital could privately acquire. The economic stasis before the expansion of capitalism, which had been calcified by inherited privileges and legacy fortunes, came to be replaced by more dynamic societies. Possibilities for social mobility created incentives for people to work harder and invest in ownership.

Undergirding this social mobility was what historian R. J. Morris, writing about nineteenth-century England, described as strategies of property.[5] More and more people took out collateralized loans and acquired marketable assets like homes,

---

4   E. J. Hobsbawm, *The Age of Capital 1848–1874* (London: Abacus, 1977); E. J. Hobsbawm, *The Age of Empire 1875–1914* (New York: Vintage Books, 1989); and E. J. Hobsbawm, *The Age of Extremes: The Short Twentieth Century 1914–1991* (London: Abacus, 1995).

5   R. J. Morris, *Men, Women, and Property in England, 1780–1870: A Social History of Family Strategies amongst the Leeds Middle Class* (Cambridge: Cambridge University Press, 2005).

government bonds and joint-stock company shares. They gave out mortgages and credit and they collected rents. If they lost their earnings they could liquidate their assets to cover the loss. The phases that marked their attainment of property shadowed the life cycles of their households. They would normally take a loan to acquire assets and to finance their sons' entry into professions and businesses. Then they would leverage their property to collect rents. This gave practical content to the values of frugality and saving, which were gaining popularity at that time. A life of leisure was nevertheless hard to come by, and the gains that new property owners attained were marred by anxiety and insecurity. But try they did for the privileges of ownership: they felt that their comfort at old age depended on it.

Scholars who study how the entire world operates as a single economic system point out that the growing wealth and proliferation of property in core countries like England in the nineteenth century would not have been possible without their domination of other countries, recast as peripheries. From colonial times onward these peripheries have been exploited in various ways to supply the core with foodstuff and raw material for industrial production, to provide cheap labor for its industry, to absorb the environmental damages of the global production processes, and to constitute a captive market for consumer goods and loans coming from the core and under its terms. The proliferation of private property in the core has been made possible by this process. That one part of the world now has broad spectrums of the population identifying as middle class, while elsewhere only a measly few can plausibly reach for similar distinction, stems from the unequal global division of labor and capital. As the surplus of capitalist production travels around the world, core states wielding greater powers in the international exchange of physical and material resources intervene to tilt its flow toward their own citizens.[6]

Private property has proven tricky even in core countries, however. In the early days of capitalism, its significance for economic growth issued from being an alternative to inherited fortunes and birthrights. It encouraged growing portions of the population to work and invest for the sake of their future, personifying in their industriousness and frugality the very opposite of rent-collecting complacency and economic stasis. But for the people who pursued ownership, sacrificing some consumption and putting in the extra effort was only worth it for the sake of being able to someday *stop* working and investing so much or to help their children do so. People wanted property to sit on, not to reinvest. They hoped to use their property to collect the rents that would help them live comfortably. A good home life, rather than the maximization of profit, was the common rationale for enterprise and private asset accumulation.[7]

The popularization of investment in household property had influential spokespeople like the nineteenth-century economist Alfred Marshall singing its praises. He advocated the state's protection of rights to own property for the sake of common well-being, and he defended property ownership against the state's infringement on these rights. Voicing the

---

6   I. Wallerstein, "Class Conflict in the Capitalist World Economy," in E. Balibar and I. Wallerstein, eds., *Race, Nation, Class: Ambiguous Identities* (London: Verso, 1991), 115–24.

7   L. Davidoff and C. Hall, *Family Fortunes: Men and Women of the English Middle Class 1780–1850* (London: Hutchinson, 1987).

optimism of early promoters of capitalism, he took for granted
that accumulation at large and people's acquisition of property
through saving and investment were codependent and inter-
linked.[8] The conflation of personal investment and economic
growth permeated ensuing generations' notion that ownership
and entrepreneurship acted as twin motors of growth.
Increasingly, however, some noticed that the very entrepreneurs who were committed to market-friendly ideals of risk,
chance and free competition transformed into market-subverting
monopolists as soon as they advanced enough to gang up and
protect their investments from intrusion by a new round of
aspirants.[9]

Sociologist Immanuel Wallerstein grappled with this paradox in his reflections on the incongruity of the designation
"middle class."[10] He traced it to an apocryphal story of the
bourgeoisie having risen to overthrow a formally dominant
aristocracy, expand the realm of monetary transactions and
unleash therein the wonders of the modern world. He couched
this story in its property equivalent of a historical evolution
from feudalist rent-seeking to industrial profit making. In
reality, this kind of temporal sequence has generally been
short-lived and often run in the other direction. Every
capitalist has sought to transform profit into rent, which is an
income higher than what a truly competitive market would
allow. Capitalism has never known widespread free enterprise

---

8   F. Boldizzoni, *Means and Ends: The Idea of Capital in the West, 1500–
1970* (New York: Palgrave Macmillan, 2008).

9   R. Goffee and R. Scase, *The Entrepreneurial Middle Class* (London:
Croom Helm, 1982).

10   I. Wallerstein, "The Bourgeois(ie) as Concept and Reality," *New Left
Review*, 1988, 167 (January–February), 91–106.

because capitalists are structurally induced to maximize their profits. Accordingly, they are ever on the lookout for monopoly positions and advantages in ownership. Their success in finding them, and the subsequent sedimentation of their privileges (Wallerstein's examples range from Thomas Mann's Buddenbrooks to aristocratization in nineteenth-century Egypt), has been deemed in literature and political theory to exemplify the betrayal of the bourgeoisie: its alleged refusal to assume the enterprising role that capitalism assigns it.

Capitalism is nevertheless personified in the ideological figure of the tireless middle-class self-improver. Wallerstein explains that, however fabricated the designation, it reappears in every interpretation of the modern world because it is hard to tell a story without its protagonist. Positing the proliferation of enterprising actors makes it easier to sell a vision of capitalism as progressive growth and development, which these actors supposedly personify. But the enterprise of the prototypical middle-class actor hits up against the rent-seeking aspirations of the same actor. Both impulses are equally endemic to capitalism, as a system that offers its actors only provisional opportunities for self-betterment. Because the dynamic of accumulation ultimately undermines these actors' goals, those in positions of power inevitably brush up against it. I want to spend the rest of this chapter fleshing this contradiction out conceptually and ethnographically, first by reading between the lines of Frank Knight and then by discussing property strategies in the West and the Rest as they touch ground.

Economist Frank Knight's *Risk, Uncertainty and Profit* is enjoying a bit of a comeback as an early defense of the kind of risk taking that is de rigueur in the contemporary moment.[11] In line with mainstream economic theory, Knight considers the economy a reflection of the interaction between numerous interest-pursuing individuals who possess material property, money or simply the capacity to work. To maximize the value of these resources, they gravitate toward social or professional groups to which they can make the largest and therefore most prized contributions. These groups, in turn, vie for advantages by courting promising members through competitive guarantees. It is a framework in which everyone has the motivation to contribute their utmost by being rewarded according to the contribution they make.

Knight attributes the dynamism of this system to the uncertainty that afflicts its actors. The price of resources bought and sold is an estimate of their productivity. Once production kicks off, conditions like supply and demand change in ways that confirm or upset initial expectations. Because the future is unknown, the cost of producing things diverges from the price at which they end up being sold. The uncertainties of production give entrepreneurs a chance to turn a profit from the difference between the amounts that competition makes them pay for the work and resources they employ, and those they can gain in the final sale of the product. These employers as well as the financiers who fund their enterprises make regular estimates regarding future profits and invest accordingly. Knight built a strong case for the economic value of ownership and uncertainty: the possibility of acquiring and owning things encourages everyone to invest despite the risks. Uncertainty

---

11   F. H. Knight, *Risk, Uncertainty, and Profit* (Boston, MA, 1921; Online Library of Liberty, 2018).

about the future animates cohort upon cohort of risk-taking entrepreneurs.[12] Without it, enterprise would grind to a halt.

Knight also recognized that people come up with ways of minimizing the uncertainties that threaten to set them back. Their efforts are aided by statistics and modeling, which guide the consolidation of many measurable ventures, a balancing out that offsets the possible failures and shortcoming of each. Producers hedge against losses by passing some of the risk on to investors. Investors also distribute risk by issuing shares, while professional speculators diversify and bet multiple times to cancel out errors. These efforts manifest widespread risk aversion. People might well take on a risk for the sake of some-day owning a portion of the wealth they collectively create, but once the wealth is accrued, they are in no hurry to let go of it. Their success is therefore realized in what, from the standpoint of economic accumulation, is a socially wasteful skimming off of the surplus and hoarding it for personal use, instead of streaming resources back into circulation.

This being the case, Knight mused, an economic system would not be efficient unless its contributors' rewards were short-lived. Only with provisional rewards would people be invigorated to promptly invest anew in the production process, placing their money back in circulation and throwing them-selves with renewed energy back to work. He doubted, therefore, whether private ownership really is the most efficient way for society to reward its members for their investments. He also questioned the wisdom of permitting risks to be

---

12   For simplicity I treat risk and uncertainty as interchangeable, although Knight is famous for distinguishing between them by relating risk to future events that, unlike uncertainties, occur with measurable probability.

undertaken individually. He even entertained the idea of restricting the freedom of ownership and risk taking "where the fundamentals of a decent and self-respecting existence are at stake."[13]

The feature of ownership that threatens the decent existence that Knight had in mind is that it gives shape to people's quest for security. To the extent that they can, those who grab hold of property try to retain it. This is a serious problem for anyone who still believes in the confluence of economic growth, which is fueled by interminable and risk-laden investments, with people's well-being, which relies on a respite from such efforts. In fact, it is a telltale sign that the economy's process of accumulation and the goals of the people who operate within it are at cross-purposes. From the perspective of people's actual behaviors, the ubiquity of property investment looks more like a compulsion performed in the absence of alternatives for attaining security than an opportunity seized upon with entrepreneurial élan.

Property's ideological underpinnings mirror those of the middle class insofar as both distill into a notion of investment. We consider investment a means by which to carve out our fortunes, and we perceive property to be the repository of the value we invest. In social environments brimming with risks and uncertainties, investment in material and immaterial property is a last-ditch reach for a better life. Much as liberal thought likes to imagine proprietary goals as self-evident, we do not invest in property for its own sake but for all the things it represents; it is a vehicle for whatever emotional, social or moral significance we attribute to it, with security as an

---

13   Knight, *Risk, Uncertainty, and Profit*, 190.

underlying baseline and the hope of prosperity a common complement.

Political scientist Debbie Becher observed popular struggles in Philadelphia around the government's takeover of private property for development under the aegis of eminent domain: the legal right of the state to appropriate private property for public use.[14] She describes how, counter to what one might expect hearing all of the libertarian rhetoric about the sanctity of private ownership, most people whose houses had been confiscated were not overly attached to the property they owned. They accepted the government's taking away what was rightfully theirs to the extent that it committed to vouchsafing the value of their investments and compensating them fairly. Having sacrificed money, time, work, emotion and relationships for the sake of their property, their utmost concern was to make sure that their efforts had not been in vain and they would land safely on their feet.

Becher also describes these people creating and maintaining neighborhood networks and organizations to make their places of residence attractive so as to raise the value of their homes, or if it comes to that, the compensation for their losses. Measures to protect and enhance the value of property are often more exclusionary. They consist, for example, of working to hinder others from getting property of a certain kind without equal investment, or attempting to prevent this property from becoming so widespread as to lose its value. We might conspire with others who own the same things as we do to undermine free competition over them, for example by supporting zoning

---

14   D. Becher, *Private Property and Public Power: Eminent Domain in Philadelphia* (New York: Oxford University Press, 2014).

laws or thresholds that exclude certain people from our neighborhoods and schools.[15] We count on our insurers to thoroughly interrogate claims and not accept just anyone into our risk pool. We resent others using our ideas, our work or even our internet connections without our being acknowledged or compensated for it. And we defend the upholding of criteria for attaining the educational or professional credentials that we have worked so hard to acquire.

It's not that we want to tighten our grip on any specific asset so much as that we wish to make our investments count. And investments only count insofar as they realize a value that is relative to that of others. When property does not improve our fortunes in any clear-cut way, we construct a fantasy land of security upon the advantages it offers us over others. We hope to gain socially and materially from the fact that, over time, other people—sometimes the very people we are forced to compete with over incomes and resources—have to expend more than we do when they do not own what we own. And we reassure ourselves that if property values come tumbling down, those with fewer resources will fall first and their bodies will cushion our own collapse.

Property strategies are not made of a single cloth. Economists associate their advantages with rents, an added

---

15   R. Heiman, *Driving After Class: Anxious Times in an American Suburb* (Oakland: University of California Press, 2015), describes a variety of "gating" practices in an American middle-class suburb. R. W. Woldoff, L. M. Morrison and M. R. Glass, *Priced Out: Stuyvesant Town and the Loss of Middle-Class Neighborhoods* (New York: New York University Press, 2016), describe struggles for security in a Manhattan neighborhood among rent-regulated tenants, market-rate tenants and new owners, and how it hastens the squeeze of the middle class.

value that people who own scarce property can charge others for its use, for example by renting out an apartment they own. Tenants, too, can try to lock in below-market rates, attaining rent value from the protections they obtain. Rents are also charged collectively and indirectly when groups organize to capture better public services and other public resources for their ethnic or religious groups or for their places of residence. People can enhance the value of their property by mobilizing economic, legal and political resources to limit the supply of or popular access to homes, schools, professional credentials, insurance pools and credit, and the social, cultural and material infrastructure of neighborhoods, towns and countries.[16]

One variant of private rent seeking is social insurance arrangements. There is a widespread misperception of social insurance as somehow opposed to property ownership, even as violating it. But social insurance is designed to maintain the continuity of incomes through bouts of unemployment, ill health or old age. Only by virtue of this kind of support can most of us hope to save and invest in property and to shore up and transmit its value to our children. Such broad risk-pooling and risk-mitigating arrangements allow us to carry large mortgage loads over decades without fearing that interruptions to our earnings will bury us under a mountain

---

16   A. B. Sorenson, in "Toward a Sounder Basis for Class Analysis," *American Journal of Sociology*, 2000, 105(6), 1523–58, proposed that class action is nothing other than rent seeking. His argument has drawn heat for presupposing a flat society in which everyone is in an equal position to compete for rent: reproducing, in effect, a middle-class ideology. B. Skeggs, *Class, Self, Culture* (London: Routledge, 2004), runs through these debates and adds biting critiques of her own.

of unserviceable debt. Social insurance also convinces banks to assume the risk of defaults, which are endemic to long-term financing for large swaths of the population. Pension funds only buy payment streams from banks and mortgage-lending agencies so long as insurance pools provide the safety nets that render working households creditworthy. This is precisely the mechanism that has historically enabled populations in advanced economies to acquire household property en masse.[17]

All of these strategies are implicated in accumulation whether we like it or not. If we own property, we want to make sure that its value does not drop so much as to rob us of security. We must therefore keep a wary eye out for others whose pursuits might compromise this value. We also have to keep sight of the forces that maintain what economists call a healthy rate of growth, which we hope might shield our property from the devastating effects of stagnation, inflation and financial crisis. This is no less true for those of us who prefer social insurance arrangements as protections and leverages for ownership. Such arrangements are highly sensitive to fiscal pressures and are the first to go when states reprioritize their budgeting. In principle, we are aligned with the process of accumulation through our various ownership precautions and aspirations.

Studying Western Europe since the Second World War, sociologist Steffen Mau shows how the income-stabilizing arrangements of social insurance have allowed large portions of its working population to buy homes, attain education, save

---

17   H. Schwartz, "The Really Big Trade-Off Revisited: Why Balance Sheets Matter," invited talk, Central European University, May 11, 2015.

money for the future and amass property.[18] These credentialed and propertied workers have subsequently learned how to invest their money in ways that would prevent its expropriation through taxation and inflation. They have also benefited from higher returns on their investment in property and assets than their earned income increases. Consequently, they are no longer as supportive of social insurance arrangements as they used to be and have instead been warming up to policies that facilitate and protect private rent collecting.

Anthropologists afford fine-grained analyses of these populations. They show how in Sweden, for example, attempts to preserve the institutional foundations of the welfare state have been reflected in people's insistence that transactions come with a receipt, as an indication of the value-added tax paid to the state; in their heated debates over who and which actions merit debt forgiveness; and in their banishment of people deemed vagrants and parasites outside the bounds of their community.[19] The liberalization of Sweden's public pension system has undercut its risk-pooling arrangements to such an extent that Swedes respond with defiance, insisting that they are ill-equipped to self-manage their savings. Even so, many of them proceed to do just that by buying stocks, private insurance policies and real estate, such that property markets in Sweden are now booming.[20]

---

18   S. Mau, *Inequality, Marketization and the Majority Class* (London: Palgrave Macmillan, 2015).

19   G. Peebles, *The Euro and Its Rivals: Currency and the Construction of a Transnational City* (Bloomington: Indiana University Press, 2011).

20   A. Nyqvist, *Reform and Responsibility in the Remaking of the Swedish National Pension System: Opening the Orange Envelope* (New York: Palgrave Macmillan, 2016). I found similar sentiments, as well as consumerist responses

In Germany, the public pay-as-you-go pension system is relatively resilient. Along with other aspects of its social insurance arrangements, it has allowed Germany's current retirees to be hailed the happiest in its modern history.[21] As part of a larger study on financialization in Germany, I interviewed recent retirees, tracing the relation of their property pursuits and protections to a middle-class ideology.[22] I found that the homeowners among them borrowed to purchase their homes, with scant regard for price development, when starting families. Fluctuations in real estate prices hit them as unexpected occurrences they neither counted on nor provisioned against. They studied and trained for professions they found interesting without much thought to employment opportunities. Their credentials won them jobs, and whenever their careers were interrupted, they could draw on unemployment insurance, child-rearing benefits and retraining programs to get back on track. Throughout their working lives, automatic deductions from their paychecks added up to claims on retirement annuities at levels that in most cases preserved their preretirement standards of living. These standards were adjusted to the resources they accrued over time through institutions like tiered public education and training programs, leading to jobs with gradated salary scales that synchronized these standards with their expectations.

---

to them, in my ethnographic work in Israel following the liberalization of its pension system: H. Weiss, "Financialization and Its Discontents: Israelis Negotiating Pensions," *American Anthropologist*, 2015, 117(3), 506–18.

21   "Die glücklichen Alten," *Der Spiegel*, March 1, 2017; "Generation glücklich," *Frankfurter Allgemeine Zeitung*, March 1, 2017.

22   I present and analyze these interviews elsewhere (H. Weiss, "Lifecycle Planning and Responsibility: Prospection and Retrospection in Germany," *Ethnos* 2018).

This protective and enabling apparatus did not minimize the inequalities that material possessions and professional credentials generated between them. The combination of protections and inequality encouraged them to place great weight on their personal efforts and investments, seeing them as having generated their different fates and status positions. Many stated that they had been schooled in frugality, and a few boasted that they had never taken out a loan. Those who had taken out loans made a point of mentioning how meticulous they were about repayment. They were all self-made as far as they were concerned. Sure, the resources that some of them received from their parents and banks made things easier, but they found them barely worth mentioning in comparison to their own undertakings. Publicly funded education and training, work protection and insurance arrangements encouraged them to develop and apply their skills, yet they considered these institutions (if at all) as background factors, while their own investments loomed large. Those who did well at school, built good social networks, attained professional skills and bought houses took pride in having had the intelligence and resolve to carve out their own fortunes.

A retired special education teacher's story is a good example of this. Aside from the modest pensions that he and his wife were receiving, their entire wealth was in their house. If ever in need of special care, they could sell it at a profit. An old barn house, they bought it long ago in a state of disrepair, financing the purchase with a loan they were almost done paying off. They only took out the loan after he had been tenured, assuring the bank that the credit would be repaid in full. They renovated the house with help from family and friends, devoting weekends and summer vacations over many years to the repair. "We produced value though our own work," he said, "and it paid off: we couldn't have afforded this house otherwise."

As was common for kids of his social background, he had been sent to vocational school, followed by training for a printing profession that no longer exists. While working, he went to night school to get a high school diploma with which he could then attend a tuition-free public university to become a teacher, as he had always wanted. He later availed himself of a public training program for teaching special education. Excelling at his job, he assumed greater responsibilities over the years, climbing up the pay grade. When reflecting back upon his life, the house came up again. "Our living standards improved steadily to the point where we live here, and live well," he said. "I'm the son of a mechanic. Today I am squarely middle class. But if I had continued doing what I was originally trained to do and had not been active, taking advantage of opportunities and doing my job well, I would never be where I am today."

Things looked quite different when I asked the retirees about their grown children, many of whom were struggling. The retirees had trouble reconciling this with the investment ethos that Germany's postwar arrangements had made credible for them. They suspected weaknesses and failings. These children, unlike their parents, have grown up in affluence and never gained an appreciation for the value of money and hard work. Faced with the dizzying temptations of consumerism (the grandchildren's embarrassment of toys is not to be believed), they are quick to take loans without saving up first. The retirees made much of the help they offered their children, sometimes contrasting it to their own proud sense of independence. If they had any concerns about their own future, these had to do with collective threats such as political developments and strains on the public pension system. But their fears for their children positioned them against the very risk-pooling and regulatory institutions that had validated their own investments. A couple whose Berlin apartment doubled in value over the past decade insisted, "This kind of real estate bubble is very bad for society, but it's good for our kids: they will get the nice inheritance they so desperately need."

Preferences for either public risk pooling or private rent seeking vary, then, with their viability under specific national-economic constellations. What remains constant is that property—whether its value is protected or not—binds its owners and pursuers to the forces of accumulation through their self-interests. We take responsibility for our fortunes by investing and by trying to make our investments count. The risks entailed in our investments are easier to swallow when we are convinced that they give us a better shot at achieving our future goals than we would have had if we refrained from investing. We expect our investments to yield fairly predictable outcomes. These outcomes don't have to be exactly equivalent to or larger than their initial value, so long as they retain a value sufficient to support our quest for security.

Yet security is precisely what property cannot deliver if the economy is to grow through unending investment and risky enterprise. In a capitalist economy, property is congenial to widespread and continuous investment: drawing capital from workers and channeling it to markets. To lure everyone in, investment has to offer real and visible rewards. But for accumulation to continue unhindered, these rewards have to be, within the bounds of political acceptability, as provisional and short-lived as Frank Knight intimated. Importantly, they cannot permit us to stop investing, and they most certainly cannot permit too many of us to sit back and collect rents.

Property baits and switches in this way because the concept is an abstraction. It is neither any given house, car or savings account, nor is it a piece of paper etched with a dollar sign, an insurance policy or an academic or professional credential. A general category that would encompass all of these things and then some, property is access to the market value they would bring in. But value, in a capitalist system, is by nature unstable. Even when we think we know the market value of our possessions, we realize that it can change at any moment without our being able to do much about it. What we own when we own property, insofar as it is identified with the value it represents, is a fraction of what all of us produce. Each fraction is relative to all other fractions, which are in perpetual flux, multiplying and subdividing according to market forces like supply and demand, and fluctuating in response to social and political forces that influence market exchanges and working conditions. We invest in property because, in its tangibility, it appears to store the value that we place in it. But since the value encapsulated in our property is outside our command, this appearance is an illusion.

We count on our fraction of stored value growing larger in relation to the aggregate, or at least not diminishing too much relative to it. We try, to the extent that we can, to hedge our bets by diversifying the things in which we invest. We struggle for, invest in and try to maintain our grip on the property we think gives us the best shot at someday retrieving at least the value we have invested in it. When in doubt, turn our sight to the advantages our property offers us in an environment whose members must always be competing over incomes and resources. When work earnings and other resources are unreliable or scarce, property appeals to us by dint of the advantages it offers those who own more of it over those who own less. These advantages often persist even when the value of property drops. Competitive advantage, embodied in property's relative value, becomes a substitute for genuine security and prosperity.

Buying into the illusion of property-as-security and aspiring to acquire more of it is a lot like being beguiled by the idea of the middle class and deploring its squeeze. More often than not, the notions of self-determined social mobility they both imply fuel the same struggles. So many social and political energies are spent on trying to lower the price of the things that make up the cost of living. The soaring prices of homes, credentials and insurance make them less accessible to growing swaths of the population. Hence the "rising cost of adequate": the standards of living that people enjoyed a mere generation ago falling out of reach for this generation.[23] Some on the political right respond by demanding the provision of credit that would help "deserving" workers purchase such things, while excluding the less creditworthy. Some on the political left respond by calling for public protections that would help many more people attain and hold on to a property threshold. Regardless of our leanings, we stubbornly hark back to property and the value it represents. Until, that is, we are left with an empty shell in the form of a house worth less than our mortgage debt on it, a pension that condemns us to poverty at

---

23   R. H. Frank, *Falling Behind: How Rising Inequality Harms the Middle Class* (Berkeley: University of California Press, 2007), 43.

old age or a credential that fails to win us a decent job. Value is where accumulation tinkers with our investments and their repositories behind our backs while we forge ahead, spellbound by the discreet charm of property.

One side effect of property's unsteady value is the resurgence of conspicuous consumption. Consumption and ownership generally move in opposite directions. Most people can only afford expensive property like a home, a pension or an academic degree by saving or servicing a loan at the expense of splurging in the present. Buying flashy things to stand out from the crowd is therefore not usually singled out as middle-class behavior, but as one more often associated with relatively successful members of lower-income groups. Those whose wealth is tenuous, it is explained, have greater need to signal their relative success through material objects.[24] But the tables are turned once precarity pervades the lives of self-identified middle classes. In her ethnographic study of suburbanites in the US, Rachel Heiman finds their insecurity translating into a conspicuous display of SUVs, high-end sports gear, ever-larger homes and eye-catching architectural ornaments.[25] The fragility of their success sets off aggressive struggles for appearance.

Critics of property ownership sometimes warn against the social and economic costs of its concentration among the few, and call for its equitable distribution. Thomas Piketty's widely

24 P. Bourdieu, *Distinction: A Social Critique of the Judgment of Taste*, trans. R. Nice (Harvard University Press, 1984); R. Burger, M. Louw, B. B. I. de Oliveira Pegado and S. van der Berg, "Understanding Consumption Patterns of the Established and Emerging South African Black Middle Class," *Development South Africa*, 2015, 32(1), 41–56.

25 R. Heiman, *Driving After Class: Anxious Times in an American Suburb*.

read *Capital in the Twenty-First Century* is a recent example.[26] He tells how at almost every point in modern capitalism except for the post–World War II decades, returns on property have exceeded the rate of economic growth, which is indirectly reflected in wage rates.[27] Property, in brief, has traditionally been a source of greater monetary value than work. People without property pay higher rents while in aggregate making less money from work than the property-generated incomes of their cohorts. It is harder for them to improve their prospects, while property owners can save and bequeath their children the resources that would help them acquire even more. Consequently, wealth becomes concentrated among the privileged and society becomes unequal and static. With limited access to property and the opportunities it affords for upward mobility, entrepreneurs turn into rent collectors, the majority of the population is bereft of the means to invest, and the economy grows at a sluggish pace.

Piketty's exposé on inequality, along with his proposal to tax property, have been amply appreciated and scrutinized. Far less attention has been paid to a particular vein in his argument: the increasing volatility of property values. He picks apart nineteenth-century novels by Honoré de Balzac and Jane Austen to show how, in extreme rentier societies, it made sense to scorn work and instead pursue estates that could be inherited or married into. Bringing in far more than anything earned from work, property gave credence to

---

26   T. Piketty, *Capital in the Twenty-First Century*, trans. A. Goldhammer (Cambridge, MA: Belknap Press, 2014).

27   He misleadingly calls it capital but actually refers in his examples to property in its various material and immaterial forms.

marriage-obsessed heroines. Back when inflation was non-existent, its value was also stable enough to generate steady incomes. Nineteenth-century novelists quoted the prices of things, assuming they would stay the same down the generations. Property these days is again concentrated and more profitable, but in contrast to the nineteenth century, it is also dynamic and volatile. Piles of banknotes are likely to disappear before one's eyes unless they are managed and reinvested. Piketty raises but summarily dismisses the significance of this volatility, claiming that people with large fortunes diversify to hedge the risk. While this may be true, the property owned by the vast majority of workers remains relatively rigid and undiversified. It is so vulnerable to value fluctuations as to no longer translate into security.

Piketty's account is symptomatic of a prevalent focus on the inequality that issues from uneven property ownership. Analysts who discuss the social impacts of what and how much people own proceed from the assumption that the higher the price of these possessions, the fewer people they can benefit. But they do not spend nearly as much time addressing the makings of property's value. It is not that inequality doesn't matter or hasn't grown: it most certainly does and patently has. But at least for the US, manifesting a trend that is arguably spreading through other economies, what has grown much faster in the past couple of decades is the sharpness with which incomes rise and fall.[28] Unstable incomes, including in the form of rents and revenues from property, ought to place the relation between value and accumulation under closer scrutiny.

28   J. Hacker, *The Great Risk Shift* (Oxford: Oxford University Press, 2008).

Concern over the inequality of ownership sometimes generates resentment against wealthy elites, but protests and reforms
that focus exclusively on the distribution of wealth without altering the conditions of its production and reproduction can only
accomplish so much. For those of us who spend less time trying
to transform society than we do planning our futures and caring
for our loved ones, hyperawareness of inequality and its effects
encourages either single-minded investment in property to stay
afloat, even when our efforts are counterproductive; social
investment meant to boost the value of our common property,
even when the personal bonds it fabricates are instrumental and
tenuous; or a chase after rents that would perpetuate our advantages over others and prevent our decline relative to them, even
when this intensifies the competitive pressure over the stuff we
all seek and does not afford us much security anyway.

Financial markets now determine the price of everything we
fully or partly own in ways that are far less intuitive than they
used to be. Banks break down property in the form of mortgage payments on our homes into small pieces, bundling them
to be sold as segmented investment products. Institutional
investors such as insurance companies, pension funds, mutual
funds and private equity firms collect our savings and invest
them in these products as well as in other enterprises. They
thereby tie our interests to them, generating mass investment
that fortifies the dominance of finance.[29] Rather than property
owners in the traditional sense, we become stakeholders in
the economy at large, either literally, by having portfolios

29   A. Harmes, "Mass Investment Culture," *New Left Review*, 2001, 9
(May–June), 103–24; P. Langley, "Financialization and the Consumer Credit
Boom," *Competition and Change*, 2008, 12(2), 133–47.

that consist of shares in firms and a claim on bundled revenues, or indirectly, through our mortgaged homes and invested savings. Our fortunes as small-time proprietors come to depend on things like corporate profits and higher interests on account balances.

The financial pooling of our investments through capital markets is meant to offset what, from the standpoint of accumulation, is a wasteful hoarding of private property, and to lower barriers on the profit-generating flow of capital. The property we own is broken up into its abstract components, invested in economic enterprise and set free to find the highest rates of return or risk being lost. It does so without our ever having steered it in those directions. In the process, work comes under mounting pressure to be productive in order to deliver the returns that shareholders demand. The more productive work is, the less work-time is required to produce the same amount of commodities. The usual capitalist dynamic follows, with the working population growing faster than gainful employment and then being confronted by capital that, lacking profitable investment opportunities, remains idle. Profits are facilitated thanks to amped-up investments whose aggregate value cannot be absorbed back into society in the form of anything we can actually use. Such imbalances lead to financial crises that wreak havoc on the value of our property and investments.[30]

No longer are we private owners of coherent, stable and visible property. Now, if we're lucky, we get to be collective

---

30   R. Martin, "From the Critique of Political Economy to the Critique of Finance," in B. Lee and R. Martin, eds., *Derivatives and the Wealth of Societies* (Chicago: University of Chicago Press, 2016).

investors in financial products in which property components are encapsulated, and whose value fluctuates according to broader accumulation trends. Our homes, credentials, insurance policies and pension savings may have all the trappings of security. Yet the investments they channel demolish the foundations that this security, if real, would rest upon. They undermine possibilities for alternative protections like stable work incomes, extensive social insurance and prevalent commons. Just as we entrust our resources to financial markets, their volatility grows and, along with it, the risks to which we are exposed. The contingencies we have to navigate while preparing for the future multiply, pushing us to invest further in property in the hopes of withstanding them. Having shredded other safety nets, this is the only precaution that remains.

Financialization throws into sharp relief the compulsive and self-defeating nature of the property strategies we undertake for the sake of our security and well-being. Anthropologists have observed this in the struggles of the people celebrated as the new global middle classes. The terms of these struggles are most conspicuous where private property has for a long time been absent and is now being reintroduced. In China, for example, the demise of public housing and concomitant rise of commercial real estate has made citizens converge in residential communities that are stratified materially and in terms of their infrastructure. This has popularized the notion of there being a new middle class, a term that in Chinese translates as the "new middle propertied strata." The homeowners of these strata employ consumer strategies to distinguish themselves from smaller investors, and they organize to increase their residential advantages by excluding others. Insecurity makes them redouble their efforts to preserve what resources they have accrued through the privatization of real estate.[31] The rising price of real estate, along with the erosion of money's value through inflation and the fear of currency devaluation, unpredictable market swings, and state interventions, sends other savers clambering to find alternative repositories for their money. These savers turn to wealth management services and financial products, but they fail to make money through them and sometimes even absorb losses. Yet just like home buyers, they persist, driven by a combination of hope and despair.[32]

Postsocialist Romania offers another example of self-defeating property strategies. There, land has returned to its former owners after the fall of socialism, but its value has dropped so much as to become a budgetary drain. Recipients of property in land were required to cultivate it, even if it ended up costing more than buying equivalent produce. Freighted with risk and debt, they ended up using their property to attain social status in lieu of material security. Not even those advantages accrued from the Caritas pyramid scheme. In the early 1990s, it drew the Romanian population into investment frenzy, backed by discourse about the formation of a new middle class.

---

31   L. Zhang, "Private Homes, Distinct Lifestyles: Performing a New Middle Class," in A. Ong and L. Zhang, eds., *Privatizing China* (Ithaca: Cornell University Press, 2008); and L. Zhang, *In Search of Paradise: Middle-Class Living in a Chinese Metropolis* (Ithaca: Cornell University Press, 2010). J. L. Rocca, "The Making of the Chinese Middle Class: Small Comfort and Great Expectations," *The Sciences Po Series in International Relations and Political Economy*, 2017, argues that such consumerist strategies are components of the Chinese middle classes' idealized social imaginaries.

32   L. Chumley and J. Wang, "'If You Don't Care for Your Money, It Won't Care for You': Chronotypes of Risk and Return in Chinese Wealth Management," in R. Cassidy, A. Pisac and C. Loussouarn, eds., *Qualitative Research on Gambling: Exploiting the Production and Consumption of Risk* (London: Routledge, 2013).

Investing in it was made appealing by skyrocketing inflation that wiped out the value of lifelong savings. Caritas brought Romanians to terms with two transitions: first, from the idea of an economy that is planned and managed by politicians to one that operates through abstract forces; and, second, from work being the only legitimate source of income to money reproducing itself through financial circuits. No one understood how their investments would bear fruit. Still, they were being trained to trust a market that operates behind their backs, indeed to entrust their savings to it. As the pyramid collapsed, they also learned that these savings could vanish. Only this time, they could no longer blame a political leadership that failed them but their own poor choices.[33]

Turning the spotlight on places like China and Romania, where private property has been reintroduced fairly recently, anthropologists make us more discerning observers of property strategies in places where they have been playing out for many decades. The success stories of our parents and grandparents, whose acquisition of material and immaterial property had aided their social ascent, give property the veneer of solidity. But its appendage of insurance policies, currency devaluations, financial crises, booms and busts, reminds us of just how fragile the foundations of property really are. These days, we are no longer as starry-eyed when taking on a thirty-year mortgage as our parents may have been, nor are we as complacent when imagining what our old age holds in store,

---

33   K. Verdery, *What Was Socialism, and What Comes Next?* (Princeton: Princeton University Press, 1996); K. Verdery, *The Vanishing Hectare: Property and Value in Postsocialist Transylvania* (Ithaca: Cornell University Press, 2003).

even if we prudently provision for it. Whatever our hopes and dreams in doing these things, we are also haunted by the fear that our prospects will be grimmer if we neglect to do them. The ideology of private property being a really good thing, much like that of a broad middle class as the population's bedrock of self-reliance, has arguably lost some of its luster. But if we are more jaded investors, we are investors nonetheless: we simply operate under constraints that are becoming more transparent.

3

All Too Human

Few studies of American suburbia have attained the fame of
Herbert J. Gans's 1967 *The Levittowners*. Situating himself in
the newly constructed New Jersey suburb Levittown, Gans
debunked popular perceptions of postwar suburbs as homo-
genous and conformist by describing the energy with which
Levittowners organized along a host of projects and concerns.
The diversity that Gans found in Levittown family, social and
religious life bifurcated, however, into a more polarized position on schools. The main draw of the community was its
opportunities for homeownership. Residents did not initially
concern themselves with schools, convinced that they would be
as satisfactory as their new neighbors whose children populated them. But while privately owned homes had not reflected
too many differences between these neighbors, schools had.
Pretty soon, the more affluent were sending their kids to
nearby private schools they considered superior, setting off
nervous salvos of private investment in education, which
worked against a community spirit. In the 1982 reprint of his

book, Gans describes visiting Levittown two decades after his original fieldwork to discover that "the community now appears to be a collection of individual households devoted entirely to their own concerns; which is like middle-class Americans anywhere else."[1]

What is it about education that heightens middle-class self-concern? In the previous chapter, I described how the institution of private property encourages workers to invest in the security it represents, in an environment where the things that everyone has to compete over are made scarce. These investments are then channeled through a financial market whose growth destabilizes the conditions that might help people achieve the security they strive for. In this chapter, I want to show how the same forces that threaten the value of workers' acquisitions in household property reinvigorate their investment in human capital. Communities come together to accrue material and human advantages and to facilitate the conversion of one to the other, thereby capitalizing on their acquisitions. Yet the pressure to invest, which underlies these initiatives, also intensifies competition among cohorts, isolates families from one another and sometimes even pits them against each other, depleting their common resources. Meanwhile, the ties that bind family members together in their pursuit of human capital are mobilized in the service of a broader process of economic accumulation. Family bonds consequently show the wear and tear of these investments' unreliable and insufficient returns.

---

1 H. J. Gans, *The Levittowners: Ways of Life and Politics in a New Suburban Community* (New York: Columbia University Press, 1982 [1967]), xvi.

To develop this argument I will begin with my own ethnographic journey. As a graduate student, I set out to examine
two Jewish settlements in the West Bank: the national-religious
Beit-El and the larger and more pluralist Ariel. Inserted among
Palestinian towns occupied by Israel since 1967, settlements are
usually perceived through a political lens that deems settlers
the premeditated enforcers of occupation and realizers of
colonial impulses. More cynical commentators have settlers
pursuing nothing loftier than private homes they could never
afford in Israel's core cities. Looking into settlers' motivations for relocating to the West Bank, I found something
more fluid: a wish to build something new, to live among the
like-minded, to have a good quality of life, a say in society,
and an environment in which to realize their values and instill
them in their children. So far insulated from West Bank
Palestinians whose own resources were being depleted by the
expansion of settlement infrastructure, settlers had comman-
deered a space in which they could think apolitically about
the fulfillment of these goals.[2]

As in Levittown, education was a trigger and turning point
for settlement growth in the West Bank. It took off in the 1970s
and 1980s following several years in which the standards of
Israel's public school system were compromised by policies that
integrated disadvantaged children without sufficient budgetary
counterbalance. New schools in distant settlements enjoyed
more generous public budgets spread over fewer students, and

---

2 My fieldwork was on the fine-motor dynamics in the Jewish
settlements, which related to those among West Bank Palestinians only
indirectly. I discussed this connection in publications that addressed the
Israel/Palestine conflict, which is not the case in the discussion that
follows.

only those whose parents had the gumption and wherewithal to relocate for their future. Most settlers I spoke to explained their move to the West Bank quite explicitly as an investment in their children's education.

In support of this aim, many settlements were initially pre-screened, ensuring that residents have at least some private resources and the power to channel public subsidies for the construction of private homes in lively communities. Early settlers were comfortable enough materially to shun consumerist ostentation and assume the semblance of being pioneers and political actors to be reckoned with. Channeling incomes from their Jerusalem- and Tel Aviv–based jobs to the new suburban hinterland, they could proceed to raise well-educated children in an environment where—sequestered from its cost to Palestinians—their social, moral or religious values would be held in high regard and sometimes rewarded with community-specific jobs and honors.

But by the time I had moved into my first West Bank apartment, the Israeli economy had long been restructured along the same market-dominated lines as most advanced capitalist ones. Cutbacks on public goods and services left their mark throughout the country, and settlements, though they enjoyed special subsidies, were not spared. Cost cutting meant that the use of existing settlement infrastructure was intensified through the crowding of settlement neighborhoods, schools and public institutions. Combined with diminishing public resources and growing pressures on gainful employment, it exhausted the leverage that had once allowed West Bank settlers to translate their material advantages into social ones.

External pressures generated internal tensions. In Beit-El, second-generation settlers were dismissive of the collective spirit to which their parents had been drawn. They either eschewed material comfort altogether for the sake of ascetic spiritual gratification on hilltop encampments or sought self-fulfillment through employment, residence and consumption in Israel proper. Their parents respectively bemoaned their failure to spare their children such renunciations or congratulated themselves (so long as their children's lifestyles did not stray too far from their own) for having provided them with the means to thrive independently. In Ariel, the esprit de corps of the early days gave way to defiant pragmatism. Each family wrested what it could from funds and donations, competed with its cohorts over advantages in schooling and housing, and resented new residents—a poorer population in the mid-eighties and Russian-speaking immigrants in the early nineties—whose arrival threatened to negatively impact the value of their homes.

My analysis of these processes amounted to a polemic against the common preoccupation with the materiality of settlements.[3] At the time I was conducting fieldwork, images of bulldozers tearing apart settlement homes in the Gaza Strip following Israel's "disengagement" from that area were still fresh in everyone's minds. Arguments raged over West Bank settlements' physical existence and the rights of settlers to their

---

3   H. Weiss, "Volatile Investments and Unruly Youth in a West Bank Settlement," *Journal of Youth Studies,* 2010, 13(1), 17–33; H. Weiss, "Immigration and West Bank Settlement Normalization," *Political and Legal Anthropology Review (PoLAR),* 2011, 34(1), 112–30; H. Weiss, "On Value and Values in a West Bank Settlement," *American Ethnologist,* 2011, 38(1), 34–45; H. Weiss, "Embedded Politics in a West Bank Settlement," in M. Allegra, A. Handel and E. Maggor, eds., *Normalizing Occupation: The Politics of Everyday Life in the West Bank Settlements* (Bloomington: Indiana University Press, 2017).

property. The state's larger intentions notwithstanding, my observations alerted me to the inseparability of material factors from social and human ones. The erstwhile convergence of creature comforts with a flourishing social life, good education and cultural facilities was the magnet that drew people to settlements. Economic pressures undermined this convergence and dissolved settlers' bonds with one another, turning them— to echo Gans—into a collection of individual households devoted entirely to their own concerns, which is like middle-class Israelis anywhere else.

My observations also sensitized me to the unexpected significance of family dynamics to life in the settlements. First-generation settlers hoped to realize their own ideals, however vague, in their children's fortunes. They considered the second generation's choices a reflection of their own. The unruly choices of second-generation settlers were therefore emotionally fraught, interpreted by parents as either redeeming the investments they had made in their children by relocating to the West Bank or as rendering these investments meaningless. Back in the field, I hadn't considered these tensions as indicative of broader trends marking the investments normally associated with the middle class. I would like to go down that path now.

Efforts to acquire educational credentials, develop skills, attain professional qualifications and forge social networks and connections stand out among the investments we make in our future. Much like savings accounts, insurance policies, real estate and other assets, they represent our hope that the value of our investments be realized in helping us, down the line, if our work incomes are interrupted. But our saved earnings are now bundled, segmented and steered into the currents of global circulation by our banks, pension funds and insurance companies. Their financial intermediation links our interests as workers who are also property owners, with the finance-led growth that promises to protect or enhance the value of our property. It provisionally unites us with fellow owners whose fortunes are similarly bound up with this growth.

Politicians speak directly to what they pronounce to be middle-class constituencies, typically comprised of workers who provision for the future by saving and borrowing. They promise to safeguard the property interests of these workers through economic stability and sustainable growth in the real estate sector, the business sector, the banking sector, the insurance industry and the pension system. Politicians' appeals are all the more insistent when such policies demand budget cuts, layoffs and austerity measures, which hurt the very people whose interests they claim to represent. The importance of private property grows apace with the intensification of these pressures and the pullback of other safety nets.

Some of us respond to these pressures with joint efforts to ensure the continued accessibility and retention of a property threshold for all citizens of our country, for example by insisting on the public protection of incomes, pooling of risks and provisioning of credit. Others among us combine in more restrictive groups to preserve and enhance the value of our property through zoning laws that set an income floor on residence in our neighborhoods, or by insisting that our country's social insurance and taxation laws spare us from having to finance claims by people who embody larger risks.

But there is one kind of asset group that sets us apart as competitors more narrowly than material property does, and more often than it brings us together as allies and

collaborators. Following Nobel laureate Gary Becker, economists call it human capital. It encompasses all of the
immaterial powers that are generated by the investments we
make in order to get greater value out of our work, property
and social interactions. These might include educational and
professional credentials, rich and useful experiences, strong
mental and physical constitutions, good and diverse skill sets,
high status and helpful social networks. They are considered
human because they become part of our very person: a
capacity in which we recognize ourselves, and which we
wield to our benefit.

Aside from the gifts of good appearance, intellect or talent
that we may or may not have been blessed with at birth, and
from the luck of being born into a well-endowed and highly
esteemed social group, the first and arguably most important
source of human capital is the so-called middle-class family. It
consists of parents with the means to support their children
materially, emotionally and intellectually, providing them with
healthy and nurturing environments, enriching their experiences, cultivating their skills, ensuring that they get a good
education and helping them put this education to good use. It
is with reference to human capital investments that the family
has been designated "the cradle of the middle class" and the
middle-class family named a "nursery of ambition."[4]

Human capital is even more recognizable a component of
the middle-class ideology than property in its material incarn-
ation, because it resonates so well with the spirit of investment.

---

4 M. P. Ryan, *Cradle of the Middle Class: The Family in Oneida County,
New York, 1790–1865* (Cambridge: Cambridge University Press, 1981); L.
James, *The Middle Class: A History* (London: Little, Brown, 2006), 4.

Money or a house tell us little about their owners. They can be handed down the generations, relieving their recipients of at least some independent exertion. Human capital, in contrast, is nontransferable—the unique achievement of each individual. What parents do is to use their own material and human resources to give their children an upper hand, a sturdy springboard from which to leap into the race and develop skills, tastes and social networks of their own. Because only skills and networks of high enough value might win the person possessing them concrete rewards, they are more of an aspirational resource than a profitable asset in its own right. Being aspirational, human capital sets off the usual middle-class exertion of extra work, time and resources with the expectation of forthcoming returns, buoyed by the conviction that one's fortune depends on this expenditure.

New middle classes are usually distinguished from the old by their preoccupation with human capital. Waves of economic restructuring have destabilized property values in advanced economies, diminishing ownership opportunities or owners' ability to make money off of rents and revenues. The better-off members of society have set out to solidify and perpetuate their advantages by other means: specifically, by translating their material acquisitions into social status and by offering their children privileged access to superior education. Countries that boast of having new middle classes locate their origins in a shift from the propertied elites of old to the promise of social mobility that would transpire through professional skills and education.[5] The new era is sometimes referred to as

---

5   See, for example D. G. Goodman and R. Robinson, *The New Rich in Asia* (New York and London: Routledge, 1996); L. Boltanski, *The Making of*

one of meritocracy, implying that a society that once smiled only upon those born into wealth has since opened its gates to anyone with brains and moxie. Because exercising these attributes is expected to pay off, it is a system that encourages everyone to invest.

The institution of human capital intensifies investments not merely because it begins afresh with the life cycle of each and every individual but also, importantly, because these investments may never end. Every person embodies some range and magnitude of human capital, which might give him or her an advantage in society and particularly in the job market. In contrast to material capital, the quantity of human capital is limitless. Yet its value is always only relative to what everyone else brings to the table. Human capital has, therefore, a built-in tendency to escalate: as good as I might be at something, there is always going to be someone better at it, and if we're competing for the same thing, I will come up short. We have to keep making human capital investments, then, not to advance so much as to keep up. For an economic system that feeds on the value produced through unrelenting,

a Class: Cadres in French Society, trans. A. Goldhammer (Cambridge: Cambridge University Press, 1987); A. Ben-Porat, *The Bourgeoisie: A History of the Israeli Bourgeoisies* (Jerusalem: Magness Press, 1999); P. Heller and A. K. Selzer, "The Spatial Dynamics of Middle-Class Formation in Postapartheid South Africa," *Political Power and Social Theory*, 2010, 21, 147–84; L. Fernandes, *India's New Middle Class* (Minneapolis: University of Minnesota Press, 2006); M. O'Dougherty, *Consumption Intensified: The Politics of Middle-Class Life in Brazil* (Durham: Duke University Press, 2002); T. Bhattacharya, *The Sentinels of Culture: Class, Education, and the Colonial Intellectual in Bengal* (Oxford: Oxford University Press, 2005); H. J. Rutz and E. M. Balkan, *Reproducing Class: Education, Neoliberalism, and the Rise of the New Middle Class in Istanbul* (Oxford: Berghahn, 2009).

resource-extracting competitive investment, human capital is invaluable.

The preponderance of human capital in social life has been criticized because the conditions under which it flourishes are not meritocratic enough. Behind the veneer of equal opportunity, privilege reigns and inequality grows. No one argued this more forcibly than sociologist Pierre Bourdieu, who examined how advantages pile up when people leverage the endowments they receive from their families toward the accrual of greater relative advantages through schooling and culture.[6]

Specifically, schools and institutions of higher education turn the favorable circumstances of childhood into catalysts of success. If born into privilege, we are sent to better schools. Our upbringing and the expectations of our families prepare us to do well in these schools and gain confidence as we do, making it easier for us to overcome obstacles that the less prepared trip up on, without losing heart or momentum. Better performance paves the path to better universities, through which more valuable credentials and qualification are within reach. They can win us better jobs with higher incomes that we can then put to good use by living among our social peers in better school districts that allow us to bestow our advantages to our children.

Meanwhile, a constellation of social, family and educational advantages also affords us the time, resources and training to

6   P. Bourdieu, *Outline of a Theory of Practice*, trans. R. Nice (Cambridge: Cambridge University Press, 1977); P. Bourdieu, *Distinction: A Social Critique of the Judgment of Taste*, trans. R. Nice (Harvard University Press 1984); P. Bourdieu, *Practical Reason: On the Theory of Social Action* (Stanford: Stanford University Press, 1998), and elsewhere.

cultivate an appreciation for the forms of art, literature and music that are treasured by those with similar preparation. The ability to "get" something that might elude the less advantaged becomes socially and even morally charged, a mark of good taste. Our socially valued tastes, habits and sensibilities, refined over years of exposure that only the lucky few can afford, make us more favorably received in circles whose members are better off. We can parlay them into positions that rely on the rich repositories they imply. If we manage to convert our cultural know how into prestigious jobs, our success is accompanied by an aura of sophistication, communicating to our surroundings that we deserve what we have.

A prime culprit of inequality, the cumulative effects of human capital ought to be addressed if we hope to live in a society that grants all of its members an equal opportunity to do well. But they also have the tendency to distract us from a much deeper problem in human capital: its contribution to a process of accumulation that undermines the goals of even the best endowed among us. With everything that is produced in society designed to serve not the fulfillment of collective needs and desires but the generation of a surplus through the population's unremunerated work and investment, the humanity of human capital is called into question.

Critical theorist Moishe Postone made the connection between the material and the human when he noted that the competition-bound production process of accumulation leads not only to an abundance of goods but also to an upsurge in the knowledge and skills required to produce these goods.[7]

---

7   M. Postone, *Time, Labor, and Social Domination: A Reinterpretation of Marx's Critical Theory* (Cambridge: Cambridge University Press, 1993).

Producers try to outperform their competitors by increasing the productivity of the work they employ. They can do so through technological innovation and more efficient workplace organization, but they can also do so by boosting their workers' skills. All of these strategies allow them to pay workers the going rate while getting more value out of their work. But the advantages they gain are short-lived: competition has other producers catching up by imitating the most successful strategies, such that the social standard of productivity is reset. The race is always on, then, for the next round of technological and organizational innovation and of skill improvement.

This raises levels of productivity in one branch after the other and, by extension, lowers the value of the commodities produced. Cheapened commodities include the food, housing, education and other goods and services that make up the socially accepted standard of living. They also include the components of productive work, namely the skills, credentials and all other elements that make up human capital, which likewise cost less to produce. Whatever employers are willing to pay for these skills, their value keeps falling below the value of the commodities to which they contribute. In other words, the stuff of human capital, which we experience as personal attributes and achievements, depreciates in the process of accumulation, impoverishing thereby our very humanity.

Impoverished humanity is encapsulated in the designation of human skills, tastes and capacities as capital: a resource in the production process whose development and deployment exceed our control. The category "human capital" only makes sense in the context of capitalist production. It is this dynamic that turns social relations, skills, tastes and capacities into standardized and measurable units, comparable and therefore replaceable with those of others, as well as with material manifestations of capital. Bourdieu called this inter-convertibility. He meant that, insofar as legal, economic and educational structures have placed the components of human and material capital in equivalent positions, one could be converted into the other. Today we describe the same formula in terms of capitalizing, as in capitalizing on skills or connections. One can capitalize, for example, on a good upbringing, by attaining a prestigious university degree; on the degree and the skills that went into acquiring it, by attaining a well-paying job; on the income from the job, by obtaining generous bank credit; on the credit, by buying potentially profitable real estate in an up-and-coming neighborhood; and on residence in this neighborhood, by attaining a helpful social network and educational advantages for one's children.

But a surplus-accumulating system like capitalism reproduces itself by precluding investments from being rewarded at their full value. Traces of exploited value can be spotted in failures to smoothly and adequately capitalize on either human or material capital by converting them into their equivalents. Gainful employment and property of solid value are hard to come by, even for those whose human capital is vast. And conversely, even very rich people cannot simply buy prestige. Rather, they have to invest heavily in a prolonged process of education and cultivation to attain the human capital that some of the not-so-rich may already possess. Human and material investments are nevertheless elicited in ways that are ever more competitive and all-encompassing. It is a climate in which everyone is compelled to make greater and more frequent sacrifices for sporadic returns.

Sociologist Hartmut Rosa defines this climate in terms of acceleration: experiences and stored knowledge falling out of date so quickly that it is almost impossible to predict which connections and opportunities for action will be relevant in the future. He calls it a slippery slope, where standing still is not possible. Whoever does not strive constantly to stay up to date finds their language, their clothing, their address book, their knowledge of society, their skills, their gear and their retirement funds outmoded.[8] Confronting downward pressure on the value of the things we invest in, we cannot but invest ever more vigorously in others. But even when our stepped-up human capital investments are successful, they are more likely to win us some kind of social credit or prestige, which we may or may not be able to cash in on down the line.

Our inability to do so is becoming the more common scenario. Examples abound, but let me stick to Bourdieu's framework and say something about education and then culture. If the credentials we get from school and university ever were entry tickets to gainful employment, they certainly no longer are. Education and training programs use accreditations to maintain income levels. They close the ranks of certain professions to the general public and demand boundary-making investments. But counter-pressure by aspiring entrants as well as educational and professional contenders for the same positions have proliferated to such a degree that, for about half a century now in many advanced economies, there has been an inflationary rise in the credential price of jobs. Credentials no

---

8   H. Rosa, *Social Acceleration: A New Theory of Modernity*, trans. J. Trejo-Mathys (New York: Columbia University Press, 2013), 117.

longer guarantee good incomes because there are simply too many of them relative to desired employment opportunities.[9]

As well, the pressure of maintaining profitability through constant innovation and quick turnaround has rendered production so flexible and the job market so precarious that skills are quickly outdated, qualifications fall out of demand, and the fashionable internships and training courses of today are dead ends by the time we are done paying for them. Meeting ever-changing job requirements necessitates ongoing investment in diverse and cutting-edge skill sets. Career ladders give way to performance-related pay while jobs are detached from cumulative seniority and status. New flexible and creative jobs are only loosely connected to prestige and remuneration. Credentials become for-profit investment products that cater to consumer demand for them, a demand that diverges from and mostly exceeds available employment. Their failure to lead to steady incomes means that more and more aspirants dig themselves into a hole of student debt they have little chance of paying off.[10]

Cultural attainments are not institutionalized in the same way as education, but they face similar predicaments. There

9   R. Collins, *The Credential Society: An Historical Sociology of Education and Stratification* (New York: Academic Press, 1979). The dearth of fitting employment for the educated is at least as acute and crushing in non-Western societies, as demonstrated, for example, by S. Schielke, *Egypt in the Future Tense: Hope, Frustration and Ambivalence before and after 2011* (Bloomington: Indiana University Press, 2015); and by C. Jeffrey, *Timepass: Youth, Class, and the Politics of Waiting in India* (Stanford: Stanford University Press, 2010).

10   Mau, *Inequality, Marketization and the Majority Class*; M. Savage, *Class Analysis and Social Transformation* (Philadelphia: Open University Press, 2000); G. Standing, *The Precariat: The New Dangerous Class* (London: Bloomsbury, 2011).

may have been a time when status was as predictable as Bourdieu described it, with exposure and cultivation bought with time and money giving expression to a refinement that fortifies connoisseurs' superiority. But so-called high culture no longer yields foreseeable rewards, and pursuits of it sometimes appear no less compulsive than pursuits of property. Critics of the postwar era Theodor Adorno and Max Horkheimer had long marveled at peoples' crowding forth to get a piece of the cultural action for fear of missing something, without knowing what that something might be. We consume culture of supposedly self-evident value at our own peril, they warned.[11]

Cantankerous commentators bemoan the declining value of cultural attainments that have been cultivated over many years. They complain about boy-men who measure themselves only by peer-group fads, and of a culture that deprives us of maturity in the form of accumulated experience, cultivated taste and slow pleasures.[12] Others pronounce the demise of snobbery: to exhibit the cultural competence that wins credit in highly regarded circles, we now have to be eclectic and even omnivorous. No longer can we sit back and enjoy the fruits of tastes we had nurtured early on. Instead, we must diversify to stay relevant, tempering our knack for classical music with pop tunes or our command of the literary canon with the latest bestsellers. Only by continuing to watch, listen, read and

---

11   T. Adorno and M. Horkheimer, *Dialectic of Enlightenment*, trans. E. Jephcott (Stanford: Stanford University Press, 2002), 131.

12   For example by R. Bly, *The Sibling Society: An Impassioned Call for the Rediscovery of Adulthood* (New York: Vintage Books, 1997); and G. Cross, *Men to Boys: The Making of Modern Immaturity* (New York: Columbia University Press, 2008).

learn—that is, by reinvesting—can we hope to nod knowingly at the next cultural reference. As with financialized property, tireless reinvestment alone might keep us from falling behind, and even then, there is nothing to assure us that our efforts will bear fruit.[13]

This reality hides in plain sight when we justify the sacrifices we make as necessary for the accrual of human capital. Economists like the term because it makes it seem as though we're all quasi-capitalists exchanging and maximizing the resources at our disposal. One implication is that if we are poor, unemployed or struggling in other ways, it's because we have invested insufficiently in education and skill development. We have high stakes in the value of the skills we do possess because we're identified with them. Our social standing (and our sense of who we are) is reflected in these cultural, educational and social attainments, as well as the self-esteem that follows.[14] Human capital therefore binds us intimately with the process of accumulation that determines the value of tastes and skills according to how conducive they are to profitability. What this concept omits, as its critics point out, is the power

13   R. Kern and R. Peterson, "Changing Highbrow Taste: From Snob to Omnivore," *American Sociological Review*, 1996, 61(5), 900–7. The predicament is global. Anthropologists describe, for example, how social standing in Nepal sets off consumerist rivalries that produce no winners (M. Liechty, *Suitably Modern: Making Middle-Class Culture in a New Consumer Society* [Princeton: Princeton University Press, 2003]), and how desires for self-fulfillment among the new rich in China conflict with their dependence on business networks and social recognition (J. Osburg, *Anxious Wealth: Money and Morality Among China's New Rich* [Stanford: Stanford University Press, 2013]).

14   M. Feher, "Self-Appreciation; or, The Aspirations of Human Capital," trans. Ivan Ascher, *Public Culture*, 2009, 21(1), 21–41.

and exploitation that go into valuing specific forms of human capital.[15] Human capital conceals our unremunerated investments, as it does the process of that generates more and more of them by pitting us against each other in a scramble over resources made scarce.

Where income and status are up for grabs, we make valiant attempts to realize the promise of human capital in the face of downward pressures on our material and immaterial acquisitions. Many of these attempts take shape as social and political strategies for promoting the inter-convertibility of human and material capital, trying to capitalize on the one in pursuit of the other. In the public sector, these attempts may include pressuring governments to set guidelines for education and guarantee that standardized schooling lead to sufficient incomes. In the private sector, they may include creating residential environments that combine good infrastructure with choice schools. Housing renovation, civic activities and schooling strategies turn choice localities into good places to bring up children. We come together and are pulled apart in these attempts, our pains attesting to their fragility. Yet we name them "community" to suggest spontaneous solidarity that itself has value we could capitalize on. This label clouds the structural forces that incentivize our efforts and limit their success.[16] The coherence of

---

15   For example, S. Bowels and H. Gintis, "The Problem with Human Capital—a Marxian Critique," *The American Economic Review* 1975, 2, 74–82; W. Brown, *Undoing the Demos: Neoliberalism's Stealth Revolution* (New York: Zone Books, 2015); B. Fine, *Social Capital Versus Social Theory: Political Economy at the Turn of the Millennium* (London: Routledge, 2001); and D. Harvey, *Seventeen Contradictions and the End of Capitalism* (New York: Oxford University Press, 2014).

16   M. Joseph, *Against the Romance of Community* (Minneapolis: University of Minnesota Press, 2002), claims that communities are formed

these communities is usually hard-won and provisional. The social decline I have witnessed in West Bank settlements can be read, in this light, as a chronicle of settlers' foretold inability to sustain such aspirations.

With human capital, as with other assets whose value is drawn out over a length of time, unreliable returns permeate the relations of the people who invested in them. It wasn't by chance that the anxieties I had witnessed in West Bank settlements revolved around original settlers' grown children. They proceeded along the path ascribed to new middle classes elsewhere, whereby the more expensive and less rewarding material advantages become, the greater the emphasis on human capital. And investments in human capital, with or without the leverage of a community, are often long-term and projected down the generations. Because human capital relies so heavily on parents' investments in their children, it infuses the emotional bonds holding families together, just as these bonds adjust to accommodate human capital investments. The intensity and uncertain outcomes of human capital investments frazzle the seams of family relations.

It is impossible to talk about human capital, then, without talking about the family. One way to observe how family bonds are reshaped by the logic of human capital is by studying families ethnographically. Global middle classes are often identified by their fixation on conjugal relations and on the raising, education and cultivation of children. They are also

as members invest in human capital and use their resources to secure greater advantages. R. Yeh, *Passing: Two Publics in a Mexican Border City* (Chicago: University of Chicago Press, 2017) demonstrates the "we" of Tijuana's middle class being sustained by creating "they"s marked by criminality and poverty.

described as bearing the weight that these pressures place on family relations and family members' ability to pursue other goals.[17] Inside-the-home ethnographies of families in the US capture the frenzied activity that revolves around the accrual of human capital and the toll it takes on family life.

The Fast-Forward Family, for example, recounts parents' worry that all of their actions, insignificant as they may seem, will affect their children's prospects.[18] The study tracks the energy-draining demands of family-centered consumer culture infiltrating their workaday lives while numerous tasks and chores demand strict time-management. Working couples deal with the emotional toll of having to divide their labor while craving acknowledgment for their contributions as well as a measure of autonomy. They also walk a fine line between wanting their

---

17   See, for example, C. Freeman, *Entrepreneurial Selves: Neoliberal Respectability and the Making of a Caribbean Middle Class* (Durham: Duke University Press, 2014); F. K. Errington and D. B. Gewertz, *Emerging Middle Class in Papua New Guinea: The Telling of Difference* (Cambridge: Cambridge University Press, 1999); H. Donner, *Domestic Goddesses: Modernity, Globalisation, and Contemporary Middle-Class Identity in Urban India* (London: Routledge, 2008); H. Donner, "'Making Middle-Class Families in Calcutta," in J. G. Carrier and D. Kalb, eds., *Anthropologies of Class: Power, Practice, and Inequality* (Cambridge: Cambridge University Press, 2015); D. Sancho, *Youth, Class and Education in India: The Year that Can Make or Break You* (London: Routledge, 2015); A. R. Embong, *State Led Mobilization and the New Middle Class in Malaysia* (London: Palgrave Macmillan, 2002); D. James, *Money for Nothing: Indebtedness and Aspiration in South Africa* (Stanford: Stanford University Press, 2015); and C. Katz, "Just Managing: American Middle-Class Parenthood in Insecure Times," in C. Freeman, R. Heiman and M. Liechty, eds., *The Global Middle Classes* (Santa Fe: SAR Press, 2002).

18   E. Ochs and T. Kremer-Sadlik, eds., *The Fast-Forward Family: Home, Work and Relationships in Middle-Class America* (Berkeley: University of California Press, 2013).

children to enjoy a carefree childhood and nervously interven-
ing in their schooling and extracurricular activities. Painfully
aware of experts' warnings against over-involvement, these
parents are so concerned about their children's success in life
that they barely consider this a matter of choice.

Busier than Ever! shines a spotlight on another set of
American families unable to slow down.[19] These families
are bogged down by logistics and coping strategies, arrang-
ing their work lives and the activities of their children. Yet
they resent such details and consider them meaningless.
The pressure to be efficient has demoralizing effects. In com-
partmentalizing different aspects of work and family life in
order to cope with pressures, these families are robbed of the
resources to link different domains and life stages under a uni-
fied moral outlook, to say nothing of the ability to reflect on
their circumstances and imagine alternatives. Rather than
making progress, the ethnographers who studied them con-
clude, middle-class family life is caught up in ceaseless time
management; a practice that may or may not prove significant
for these families' futures.

Anthropology can also relativize the seeming lack of alternatives that comes with frenzied activity. It does this by
observing the things we take for granted at the very junctures
in which they have been molded. Jane Collier's ethnographic
study of a village in southern Spain uncovers some of the
forces that have transformed family relations.[20] Collier did

---

19 C. N. Darrah, J. M. Freeman and J.A. English-Lueck, *Busier than Ever! Why American Families Can't Slow Down* (Stanford: Stanford University Press, 2007).

20 J. F. Collier, *From Duty to Desire: Remaking Families in a Spanish Village* (Princeton, N.J.: Princeton University Press, 1997).

ethnographic fieldwork in Spain as a young woman in the 1960s and then returned two decades later for more fieldwork in the same village, to find it transformed. In the sixties, the village economy revolved around agriculture. Property in land was the villagers' main bulwark against the economic pressures they were experiencing at the time. Different property endowments were the reason that some were weathering these pressures better than others. But by the eighties, agriculture no longer offered viable incomes and the village had lost half of its inhabitants. They had moved away to cities to study and pursue formal occupation in what had become a more intensely capitalized economy.

The villagers born in the early decades of the twentieth century attributed the fate of their families to what each member had inherited, the fortune they married into and how they managed their property. Members of the same families who were born later in the century explained their fates in terms of the jobs they attained. By the eighties, even the wealthiest residents had to work, and they credited their work with making them wealthy. Indeed, anyone who did well insisted that this was because of their skills and the quality of their work, including those who got their jobs thanks to personal connections. Others were told that they could improve their lot if they increased their productivity. Villagers and former villagers embraced this belief, even as most of them were aware that Spain's larger networks of employment and status disadvantaged them relative to citizens growing up at its urban centers.

These economic transformations changed family relations and patterns of thought. In the sixties, village children were largely ignored unless they misbehaved: parents were singularly preoccupied with preventing their children from behaving in ways that might harm their chances of marrying someone with at least an equal inheritance. But by the eighties, human capital became the dominant means of getting ahead in life and families had become child-centered. It now behooved parents to cultivate their children's skills and sensibilities. These children came to experience themselves as expressing unique desires and abilities that could potentially be channeled into productive activities. They felt freer and less bound by convention than their parents had been.

These changes heightened the pressure to do well amid unfavorable circumstances. In the 1960s, a family's property remained under the control of parents until their deaths. The economic interests of parents and children coincided in protecting and enhancing it. In the 1980s, parents lost control over the money spent on schooling, as children could pursue goals other than those their parents encouraged. Collier writes about parents who, rather than demanding respect from their children as their own parents had, now hoped to exert influence by earning their children's affections. She dwells on the position of mothers, supposedly liberated from older patriarchal traditions. Yet they have grown far more dependent on their husbands' higher earning power than their mothers had been on the husbands with whom they shared property. Women now had to worry about their husbands' health and happiness as much as they had to worry about their children. At the same time, marriage became a fragile project one ought to constantly work on, rather than a stable institution to which one must resign oneself. Additionally, adult men and women found themselves trying to reassure their parents that they would care for them in their old age. The elderly feared abandonment and saw their children's protestations of love as so much evidence of them putting personal desires above the far more reliable sense of duty to the family.

Everywhere, human capital investments gain importance the harder it is for parents to transmit their advantages through material property. But barring sudden upheaval to property values, outcomes of material bequests are easier to foresee and control. Human capital is different. Standing in for one's person, it is always in flux. Parents cannot simply fork over human capital to their children. They have to invest over many years in their children's education and cultivation, and these are only building blocks that require further investments by the children themselves. The outcomes of these investments, materializing piecemeal over decades and subject to these children's whims no less than to economic currents, are highly unpredictable. As human capital investments flow down the generations, they mold family relations and are, in turn, molded by them.

There has been a lot of talk in recent years about the importance of the family growing apace with the withdrawal of the public resources that young adults used to draw on to get ahead in life, such as subsidized housing and education. Scholars once compared national welfare systems by the degree to which they supported de-familialization, or individuals' financial independence from their families. Others now identify the opposite in re-familialization.[21] Thirtysomethings moving back into their

---

21   L. Flynn and H. Schwartz, "No Exit: Social Reproduction in an Era of Rising Income Inequality," *Politics and Society*, 2017, 1–33; N. Oelkers, "The Redistribution of Responsibility between State and Parents: Family in the Context of Post-Welfare-State Transformation," in S. Andersen and M. Richter, eds., *The Politicization of Parenthood* (Dordrecht: Springer, 2012); A. Roberts, "Remapping Gender in the New Global Order," *Feminist Economics*,

parental homes, to mention one talked-about example, are living proof of how difficult it has become to make it without family support. The difficulty is masked by talk of family values. Championing family love and responsibility along with their correlates of household debt and collateral, this rhetoric allows families who can pool their resources to justify their advantages. It also encourages people with meager resources to appeal to their families for financial help rather than making demands on the public purse.[22] Responding to economic and emotional pressures, parents invest in their children now more than ever, but the one-time nursery of ambition has been humbled.

Pressures on the family have burst into public consciousness in Israel following a widely debated survey showing a staggering 87 percent of Israeli parents helping their grown children, who sometimes have families of their own, with regular payments and ad hoc expenditures, for which they have been pronounced the oxygen tank of the middle class.[23] Curious about the influence of family investments on family relations, I observed them in their idealized form, disseminated by the most powerful agency of contemporary capitalism: the finance sector. My angle was its ideological arm: financial literacy programs. People are instructed to manage their finances and assume responsibility over the outcomes of their financial decisions. Never mind that in financialized economies, they usually have no choice but to take on debt and invest, and scant control over the outcomes of these investments, clever as they may be

2009, 15(4), 168–72.

22 M. Cooper, *Family Values: Between Neoliberalism and the New Social Conservatism* (New York: Zone Books, 2017).

23 K. Z. Harari, "Hachamtsan hasodi shel ma'amad habeyna'im: yesh lanu cheshbon im hahorim," *Calcalist* July 27, 2013.

in making them. But of course, that's the point: preparing them to shoulder a burden they would rather do without.

The things we work hardest to attain are put at risk through adjustable-rate mortgages that determine the price we end up paying for our homes, institutionally mediated investments that threaten the value of our retirement savings, and crisis-prone markets that affect our jobs, savings and possessions. In so volatile a climate, financial education is an investment we are all encouraged to make. It is offered in public and private forums such as websites and advice columns, workshops and seminars at schools, workplaces and civic centers, or—as most common in Israel—in popular magazine articles and TV shows.[24]

Tracking the fortunes of people struggling with their finances while experts steward them toward financial enlightenment, the TV programs are all about families. Single-person households are never addressed, diverging as they do from the ideal that is projected. This ideal is spelled out in a number of ways, including in the programs' attention to children, the adorable and needy impetus for their parents' investments. Parents go along with consumption cutbacks proposed by consultants—cutting their credit cards in half and canceling their cable subscriptions—in order to help their children get ahead in life and to leave something behind for them. This something is usually a house, whose value is never calculated in terms of the money poured into it over so many years of mortgage repayments.

---

24   I followed a series of news reports, "Mishpacha Betsmicha," published in the daily *Yediot Achronot* and in ynet.co.il between 2012 and 2016; a primetime TV show, *Mishpacha Choreget* with a six-season run between 2008 and 2012; another primetime TV show, *Chayim Chadashim*, featured in 2015; and a range of advice columns on the websites of Israel's main media sources.

Children are also the stimulus for embracing the risks of enterprise and shouldering the burden of long-term saving. Parents' love for their children, the backdrop for everything else that happens in these programs, is stoked and applauded.

Just as, at various points in history, religion served to placate victims of social injustice by deferring the settling of scores to the afterlife, via children, returns on investment are deferred to an indefinite future, distracting parents from their possible insufficiency. In lieu of detailed estimates of advances and returns, parents are moved by the prospect of giving their children a better life. When or how this betterment will come about is up in the air.[25] Still, parents know that without investments in education and housing, their children risk being disadvantaged compared to the children of others. Financial advice translates their concerns into guidelines for financing their children's future through the usual channels. It is a powerful means of getting people who might otherwise squander or hoard their money to place it in circulation instead.

Marital relations, in contrast to parental ones, are represented as brittle and explosive. Couples bicker and fight, hurl accusations at each other or wallow in resentful silences, but they also try, and sometimes manage, to rekindle their love, if only for an episode or two. There is never much of a

---

25 Jeffrey, *Timepass: Youth, Class, and the Politics of Waiting in India*; M. Doepke and F. Zilibotti, "Social Class and the Spirit of Capitalism," *Journal of the European Economic Association*, 2005, 3(2–3), 516–24; S. Schielke, *Egypt in the Future Tense: Hope, Frustration and Ambivalence before and after 2011* (Bloomington: Indiana University Press, 2015); S. Jansen, *Yearnings in the Meantime: "Normal Lives" and the State in a Sarajevo Apartment Complex* (New York: Berghahn, 2015); and other anthropologists have made connections between global middle classes and waiting for a better future.

distinction between their struggles for financial success and those for marital success. The most important decisions they make—to stay together, have children, buy a house, move someplace else, work or vacation—are weighed as investment strategies. Their success hinges on the same qualities that come into play in the financial sphere: responsibility, foresight and resourcefulness. Marriage itself is made out to be an investment. Flashbacks to the relationship's beginnings paint a picture in which people marry someone who embodies future security or prosperity. Married life features as a decades-long struggle to realize this promise. If it is not realized, the spouse is a disappointment.

Spouses are confronted with their interdependence through contrived scenes in which they try and fail to manage some household task on their own or to take over the role that their spouse usually plays. Taught that they need one another, they are instructed to adjust their jobs and household responsibilities, consolidate bank accounts and invest in each other's business initiatives. Taking on a thirty-year mortgage to buy a house and raising children with decent human capital takes at least two committed, working investors. Couples are taught to accept this and invest as a joint venture, moved by their sense of responsibility to their children, first and foremost, but also to the spouse who, by choosing to marry them, has staked a claim on the potential worth of the marriage.

Other relatives are treasured insofar as they encourage rather than discourage investment and calculated risk taking. Needy relatives are drains and liabilities. But among the Israelis featured in these programs, relatives more often provide valuable resources ranging from loans and gifts, through childcare and temporary housing, to collateral on loans. If their help makes married couples lackadaisical, relatives are portrayed as obstacles to independence and adulthood. But if these relatives are catalysts for initiative, for example by guaranteeing the couple a loan for a new business or by helping them with the down payment on a house, they are welcomed as an integral part of the family and assembled to plot its financial course.

Recall the tensions that Collier identified among Spanish villagers surrounding uncertain returns on investment in spouses and children. Similar anxieties make an appearance among Israeli families as well. Financial advisors identify their debilitating effects and pilot sentiments in more investment-friendly ways. The contingency of family and marital relations is key. It shadows the contingency of the middle class: an ideology of self-determined social mobility that casts distressed workers as willing investors. Just as one's position in society cannot be static if accumulation is to expand through unending contributions, so relationships cannot be built on the bedrock of duty and tradition if they are to fuel economic growth. Instead, people's most intimate relationships—to their spouses, parents or siblings—must rest on foundations so shaky that they need to be cultivated, indeed "invested in" to realize their nested potential.

Love and devotion take center stage insofar as they inspire investment in property and human capital. Material and immaterial possessions channel the resources that spouses and parents expend from the confines of the household to the institutions of the global market, which determine their value. Because family relations are fragile, and because expenditures by family members generate unpredictable returns, investments in spouses and children, must be ongoing, feeding accumulation.

I began this chapter by observing how material decline in West Bank settlements was reflected in intergenerational anxieties. I hope by now to have established that this connection, which also characterizes the aspirational investments of other communities and families, stems from attempts to increase and capitalize on human resources. These efforts are doomed to insufficiency because they emerge out of the economy's imperative to produce a surplus, which exceeds potential rewards. If the ideology of the middle class describes our proclivity as dominated workers to nevertheless identify as self-determining investors of work, time and resources, then human capital is its most intimate manifestation. Operating as an incentive to seek advantages and guard against disadvantages in a competitive environment, it brings us to terms with a process of accumulation that commands our everyday activities and infiltrates our closest relationships. It does so by representing the inhuman capital that so dominates our lives and activities as if it were an aspect of our personality, which we are free to wield to our benefit but cannot rely upon to yield intended outcomes. It characterizes it, that is, as all too human.

4

Goodbye Values, So Long Politics

In the previous chapters, I made a case for the middle class being an ideology. It obscures the devaluation of work, and the plight of a population that suffers the consequences of this devaluation, by shifting the limelight to social mobility in the guise of investment-driven self-determination. This ideology is most credible among those who, while having to work for a living, can nevertheless devote some extra work, time and other resources toward the future, expending more than they immediately consume. Being designated "middle class," they are encouraged to think of these expenditures as choices and of their fortunes as their outcome. In a competitive environment where valuable resources are made scarce and where lasting benefits are hard to come by, such investments and the advantages they give some over others are the go-to explanations for why some people do well while others lag behind. Those who subscribe to them have good reason to redouble their efforts in order to protect what they have, obtain what they don't and generally look out for number one.

Strikingly, however, scholars who take the global middle classes as their subject matter characterize the groups so identified as the most politically active among the world population.[1] This in itself is not surprising: workers with the wherewithal to invest also have the wherewithal to protest. Given social decline and the environmental degradation that follow the exploitation of work and natural resources, there is no shortage of things to protest against. Vulnerabilities vary widely across social groups such that some suffer the injuries of global accumulation much more than others. Still, they afflict most people around the world, crossing divides of race, gender and nationality. There is therefore a strong argument to be made for protests representing an aggrieved 99 percent—a category whose broadness harmonizes with that of the idealized middle class. But what happens when protests are caught up in the ethos of self-determining investment that characterizes this middle class?

In this chapter, I take a closer look at the politics and values that match the middle-class ideology. Touching on protest and civic movements as well as on critical thought about the politics that capitalism gives rise to, I follow several articulations of politics and values in the US, first, and then—by drawing on my own ethnographic research—on their manifestations in Germany and in Israel. These examples will demonstrate various ways in which the middle-class ideology of investment-driven self-determination works against activists' farthest-reaching goals.

---

1   For example, G. Amoranto, N. Chun and A. Deolaliker, "Who Are the Middle Class and What Values Do They Hold? Evidence from the World Values Survey," *Asian Development Bank Working Paper Series*, 2010, no. 229.

It seems only right to begin with the recent spate of global protest movements, which political scientist Francis Fukuyama analyzed as constituting nothing short of a middle-class revolution.[2] He attributed the uprisings in places like Egypt, Tunisia, Turkey and Brazil to the rise of a new global middle class. Most of the protestors in these places were neither wealthy elites nor impoverished underclasses but rather young adults who had already invested in education or the acquisition of employable skills, and in some cases also in property. They resented the political reality whereby their expectations for subsequent employment and material advance had not been met. As aspirational investors, they had a lot to gain from the formulation and enactment of good policies. And insofar as their governments could confiscate their possessions and nullify their investments, they also had something to lose by the perpetuation of bad ones.[3]

Fukuyama's optimism regarding a middle-class ascent, buoyed by his belief in the investment-validating policies he saw the recent protests as advocating, is tempered by what he considered their failure to bring about the advances they envisioned. The protests had, in some countries, succeeded in toppling corrupt regimes, allowing market forces to pilot societies from within after having been inflicted on them top-down by the decree of dictators. Fukuyama is loath to attribute the

---

2 F. Fukuyama, "The Middle Class Revolution," *Wall Street Journal*, June 28, 2013; F. Fukuyama, *Political Order and Political Decay: From the Industrial Revolution to the Globalization of Democracy* (New York: Farrar, Straus and Giroux, 2014).

3 For a similar analysis of the disaffections driving the Arab Spring, see S. Devarajan and E. Ianchovichina, "A Broken Social Contract, Not High Inequality, Led to the Arab Spring," *Review of Income and Wealth*, 2017.

lack of improvement in the fortunes of their populations to such developments. He prefers to blame it on what he considers middle classes' broad alliances with non-middle-class majorities in those countries. In contrast to the market-friendly interests he assigns the middle class, he associates these majorities with protectionist agendas that ended up winning the day.

Accounts of developing economies lend support to the charge of protectionism, regardless of which social actors it is attributed to. They point to the weakness of work-related institutions and to the low rates of formal employment in these countries. Without these social arrangements, disgruntled populations lack the institutional backing for sustained resistance. Politics in developing economies have therefore taken shape in large part as struggles over property rights and protections. The people who have managed to escape poverty by accumulating property and prestige have been more likely to defend their gains against infringement by powerful elites or populist rulers. This, while the plight of the poor has been addressed through welfare measures that solidified their subordination. Income growth in those countries is therefore anything but a march toward democracy. The better endowed among what Fukuyama and others identify as global middle classes engage in distributional struggles against compatriots who are a touch more vulnerable. They demand order and stability rather than political rights across the board.[4]

---

4   A. Sumner and F. B. Wietzke, "What Are the Political and Social Implications of the 'New Middle Classes' in Developing Countries?" *International Development Institute Working Paper*, 2014, 3; and "The Developing World's 'New Middle Classes': Implication for Political Research," *Perspectives in Politics*, 2018, 16(1), 127–40. For ethnographic accounts of political sentiments caught up in these dynamics, see: A. Bayat,

Such perspectives take pains to dispel the notion that there might be anything self-defeating about the politics of capitalism's protagonists. But some of the most formidable minds in political thought have long ago hinted that this might well be the case. In 1919, sociologist Max Weber lectured student unionists in Munich on what it takes to be politically engaged. The inevitability of violence resounds through "Politics as Vocation," the essay based on his lecture notes.[5] Revisiting political movements of the past, Weber observed two different types of motivations. Politics can be driven by conviction:

"Plebeians of the Arab Spring," *Current Anthropology*, 2015, 56 (Suppl. 11): S33–S43, on middle-class protesters in Egypt making claims on resources while eschewing demands for self-governance; K. Fehervary, *Politics in Color and Concrete: Socialist Materialities and the Middle Class in Hungary* (Bloomington: Indiana University Press, 2013), on Hungarian middle classes' quest for normality used to endorse political and economic policies; L. Giesbert and S. Schotte, "Africa's New Middle Class: Fact and Fiction of its Transformative Power," *Social Science Open Access Repository* 2016, on political lethargy among African middle classes' upper strata exacerbating the frustrations of its lower ranks; M. O'Dougherty, *Consumption Intensified: The Politics of Middle-Class Life in Brazil* (Durham: Duke University Press, 2002), on consumerist aspirations trumping middle-class alliances in Brazil; A. Wedeman, "Not in My Backyard: Middle Class Protests in Contemporary China," in L. L. Marsh and L. Hongmei, eds., *The Middle Class in Emerging Societies: Consumers, Lifestyles and Markets* (London: Routledge, 2016), on middle-class protests in China focusing on apolitical "not in my backyard" issues; T. Trevisiani, "The Reshaping of Cities and Citizens in Uzbekistan: The Case of Namangan's '"New Uzbeks,"' in M. Reeves, J. Rasanayagam and J. Beyer, eds., *Ethnographies of the State in Central Asia: Performing Politics* (Bloomington: Indiana University Press, 2014), on apolitical conformism among new Uzbek middle class; and S. A. Tobin, "Jordan's Arab Spring: The Middle Class and Anti-Revolution," *Middle-East Policy*, 2012, 19(1), 96–109, on anti-revolutionary sentiments among middle classes in Jordan.

5   M. Weber, "Politics as Vocation," in D. Owen and T. B. Strong, eds., *The Vocational Lectures* (Indianapolis: Hacket, 2004).

unshakable beliefs pursued at all costs. Conviction-based politics are intoxicating, but more often than not, they lead to calamity and bloodshed. Politics can also be driven by a sense of responsibility toward the social outcomes of one's actions. Endeavors aimed at bringing about a common good are contravened, however, by the coercive means deemed necessary to implement this vision. No one who wants to engage in politics, Weber warned, can afford to ignore these paradoxes.

In the descending doom of the 1930s, German-Jewish critical theorist Max Horkheimer penned the essay "Egoism and Freedom Movements."[6] He would not have seen the paradox that Weber stipulated, whereby values conflicted with reality, and political aspirations could not be implemented other than by force, as preordained, but rather as a symptom of what he called bourgeois society. In a capitalist mode of production, people can only satisfy their needs by exchanging their physical and material resources. Artificial scarcity, brought about by producing and pricing things in a way that would maximize profit, places people in competition with one another over everything from housing and education, through a range of commodities and services, to jobs and prestige. These things can be attained with work and property incomes—earnings and assets whose value is likewise decided by competition. Bereft of collective means of support, people are isolated as individual bearers of self-interest, forced to fend for themselves in these transactions. Caring or hostile as they might be toward

---

6 M. Horkheimer, "Egoism and Freedom Movements: On the Anthropology of the Bourgeois Era," in M. Horkheimer, *Between Philosophy and Social Science*, trans. H. G. Fredrick, M. S. Kramer and J. Torpey (Cambridge: MIT Press, 1993 [1936]).

each other, their necessary exchanges of privately owned resources places them in positions of mutual indifference in their daily quest to sustain their households. In this environment, thriving or even just getting by demands no small measure of egoistic prioritizing.

This prioritizing is no fun at all, seeing as lasting pleasure and security eludes the majority of the population. People perform the work and undertake the exchanges they do because they are so compelled by the structures and institutions that organize the ownership, production and circulation of resources. They can be more efficient and economical in their undertakings if they assume a dry and instrumental sort of egoism, which substitutes the pursuit of pleasure with sedate resignation. Being competent players in the capitalist game means repressing hedonistic appetites in the service of market-determined self-advancement, a politically determined common good, or just for the sake of it: a modicum of self-denial considered a virtue in its own right.

Isolation and competition generate conflict, however, not only between people but also within each psyche, whenever a person is not so keen on being as self-concerned as circumstances call for. Philosophy, religion and ethics (Horkheimer analyzes dominant schools of thought) reflect this inner strife. On the one hand, people are comprehended in terms of the attitudes that capitalism impresses upon them, presumed innately self-serving and opportunistic in pursuit of their interests. On the other hand, any contrary disposition they display, because it appears to overcome their egoism, is consecrated as virtue and held up as an exemplar for others. People come, in this way, to measure themselves in light of moral principles that are the very opposite of what necessarily becomes of them, undermining themselves with unrealistic idealism.

Horkheimer traced the entanglements of egoism, self-denial and idealism in political movements like those associated with the Reformation and the French Revolution. The elites leading these movements, powerless to overthrow feudal or monarchical powers on their own, had to recruit the less fortunate to fight their battles for them. Promising better conditions for the masses, the policies they ended up implementing were all about bolstering capitalism by overturning corrupt leadership while expanding private ownership and making administration more efficient. As progressive as these policies may have been compared to the hierarchies that preceded them, they redefined rather than eradicated inherited inequality. No longer a matter of social status, it was now entrenched in the gap between the lucky owners of property and the propertyless majorities. For most of the population, fighting for bourgeois freedoms meant joining the fight against their own well-being.

The ambiguity of these politics crystallized in their humanist ideology. Humanism glorifies humans as creators of their destiny. It ascribes dignity to people's self-determination, their power to act in the world and tack upon their own lives. Yet the same people championing humanism and aspiring to embody it are subject to countless constraints as they navigate market dynamics that govern their use of resources and expose them to depreciation and loss. In Horkheimer's bleak judgment, "each hour society proves anew that only the circumstances, not persons, actually deserve respect."[7] The farther

---

7   M. Horkheimer, "Egoism and Freedom Movements: On the Anthropology of the Bourgeois Era," 51.

humanist ideals are from lived experience, he ruminated, the more pitiful must people appear to themselves.

Much has changed in the centuries that separate the movements of destitute masses that Horkheimer was writing about, from those that make headlines nowadays, comprised of what scholars call "the middle masses" or "the majority class."[8] Self-denial has been toned down a notch while sacrificing for the common good has fallen out of fashion. Yet the uncomfortable coexistence of egoism and humanism, self-interest and idealism seems more resilient than ever. Following Weber and Horkheimer, we can make sense of these ideals by reflecting on the structures of employment, ownership and exchange from which they grow.

A fitting prequel to this exploration is historian Lawrence Glickman's study of workers in the United States since the late nineteenth century.[9] After waves of industrialization forced them to abandon their farms and workshops to work for others, their erstwhile quest to become independent producers dissipated. Male workers grew to accept what they used to consider "wage slavery," first by necessity, and later on by moderating their expectations. Giving up on economic independence, their new cause was to make sure that they received what they called a living wage, that is, remuneration that would meet their needs as breadwinners and consumers.

Political reorientation did not stop there. Until the post–Second World War era, a living wage was calculated to enable

---

8   G. Marshall, "A Dictionary of Sociology"; S. Mau, *Inequality, Marketization and the Majority Class* (London: Palgrave Macmillan, 2015).

9   L. B. Glickman, *A Living Wage: American Workers and the Making of Consumer Society* (Ithaca: Cornell University Press, 1997).

these workers to support families, maintain self-respect and have the means and leisure to participate in civic life. But having traded off independence in production for greater access to consumer goods, workers now relied on the market alone for the fulfillment of their material needs. They could no longer resist the structures of employment and distribution from its margins. Locked in competition, they subdivided into interest groups and reconsidered their aims. The living wage was redefined downward for the less privileged as minimum wage, whereas the more privileged demanded incomes that would buy them more stuff. Glickman tells how business leaders, recognizing the economic advantage of mass consumption, welcomed such aspirations, while workers-turned-consumers eschewed political participation.

The common ground forged between workers, employers and business leaders around consumption-based living standards shaped workers' struggles in other countries as well. The terms of these alliances were rewritten after workers gave up their most ambitious demands, usually at the point in which their power to make them diminished. Social security is the best-known example. After the Second World War, Western democracies needed to prop up their economies against the backdrop of depression and the threat of communism. The welfare arrangements they instituted were an outcome of workers' demands for a sustained standard of living, combined with new strategies for enhancing profitability through workers' appeasement and transformation into consumers. Workers' savings were channeled through social insurance towards investments that fueled demand: bolstering incomes, providing employment and funding development. These arrangements remained in force until a combination of high employment and high demand placed too great a pressure on corporate profitability. From the 1970s onward they were abandoned, to degrees that varied by country, in favor of financial deregulation, privatization and the withdrawal of public protections. Workers' unions were broken and their bargaining powers truncated, while firms were forced to operate efficiently by devaluing work and making many workers redundant.[10]

In the US, where one's position in society has long reflected and reinforced consumption choices, unprotected workers are trapped in a political quagmire: the same structures that cheapen the products and services they rely on to maintain their lifestyles are bound up with those that devalue their work. The multinational retail corporation Walmart epitomizes this entanglement. Wherever it expands, prevailing wage rates are depressed. Yet it asks workers to forgo better wages in order to serve the broader societal goal of lower prices for everyone, including for their own families. Walmart has managed to convince large swaths of the American public to engage in a national conversation about a supposed trade-off between low prices and low wages. This framing not only encourages people to think of their interests solely as consumers, but it also represents the emphasis on affordable consumption as patriotic.[11]

---

10   R. Blackburn, *Age Shock: How Finance Is Failing Us* (London: Verso, 2006); G. Clark, *Pension Fund Capitalism* (New York: Oxford University Press, 2000); A. Glyn, *Capitalism Unleashed: Finance, Globalization, and Welfare* (New York: Oxford University Press, 2006); R. Pollin, "Resurrection of the Rentier," *New Left Review*, 2007, 46 (July–August), 140–53; J. Quadagno, *The Transformation of Old Age Security: Class and Politics in the American Welfare State* (Chicago: University of Chicago Press, 1988).

11   J. Collins, "Walmart, American Consumer-Citizenship, and the Erasure of Class," in J. G. Carrier and D. Kalb, eds., *Anthropologies of*

Consumer interests bind American workers to corporations and markets, which provide the resources that would help them attain expected standards of consumption and provision for the future. This alliance cuts through collective priorities and redistributive policies, further eroding the rights and demands of citizenship. Consumption marks people's position in society by signaling difference, individuality and personal aspiration. These orientations, in turn, erode their collective powers and common interests. This makes it even more remarkable that there have been social uprisings in the US of the magnitude of Occupy Wall Street. But the aspirations of inclusiveness and unity expressed in Occupy Wall Street overlaid divisions among protestors in their positions as consumers and investors. Ultimately, these divisions allowed common causes to be hijacked by consumerist, neoliberal and development narratives that diminished the uprising's collective force.[12]

If Max Weber made an analytical distinction between an ethic of conviction and an ethic of responsibility, anthropologist Joel Robbins draws attention to the circumstances that recommend each.[13] Taking responsibility over the consequences of one's actions makes sense in settings stable enough to make these consequences predictable. But these days, our

Class: Power, Practice, and Inequality (Cambridge: Cambridge University Press, 2015).

12   J. Hickel, "Liberalism and the Politics of Occupy Wall Street," *Anthropology of this Century*, 2012, 4; M. Nunlee, *When Did We All Become Middle Class?* (London: Routledge, 2016), traces, for the US, a shift from broad social and economic concerns through interest group politics to the notion that everyone is middle class because they live in a meritocracy.

13   J. Robbins, "On the Pleasures and Dangers of Culpability," *Critique of Anthropology*, 2014, 30(1), 122–8.

grandest actions are entangled in institutional realities that guide their manifestations and repercussions in ways that we may not have imagined. We are therefore more coherently attuned to clear guidelines about what constitutes virtue or vice. Robbins shows this happening among religious converts, but they are only an extreme case of a general rule: the spirit of our time is to look inward for moral guidance rather than to wade through the muddy waters of political programs whose outcomes spin beyond our control.

In trying to secure our futures and care for our families, we invest in property and human capital whose advantages are relative to what others possess. When we care for the people closest to us out of love or for those further away as a conscious and conscientious choice, we operate with an awareness of the renunciations this forces us to make. There is self-denial in choices that surpass pragmatism and utilitarianism, and it weighs heavily on these choices and colors their meaning. Freedom of choice, in a capitalist context, is exercised in the face of contravening pressures. One way that remains for us to follow our moral compass is to insist on ethical positions we can reasonably enact, those with immediate and self-exonerating effects, and whose integrity is directly validated by self-denial, while eschewing costly undertakings that seem naïve and far-fetched.

Faced with precarity, want of opportunity, flimsy protections and lower standards of living, it behooves us to take responsibility over our loved ones and devote our time and resources toward provisioning for the future. Some of us are nevertheless socially and politically active on a smaller scale. Presumed middle classes are associated not only with political protest but also with value-based volunteerism and civic activism. They are the main actors in classical studies of values in the United States.[14] As with protests and uprisings, it stands to reason that people with the means to do something for those in need would in fact do so. Like politics, however, activism within the ideological framework of the middle class takes on a peculiar form.

We like to imagine the world around us as somehow reflecting our moral values. It is what we assume when we associate the attributes of a given community—say one that is religious, multicultural, consumerist, liberal or conservative—with the values of its residents. But closer inspection never fails to reveal residents' dispositions straying from those on public display. Such incongruity can be jarring when the people in question are free to speak their minds. The tension between personal views and the morally charged structures in place is no fluke, however, but a feature of values themselves.

Freedom is believed to have been a rare luxury in precapitalist societies, where people had to bow to the demands of powerful rulers and comply with the laws they had put in place. Centralized powers and hierarchies also decreed what goods would be produced in these societies, how they would be used and under what terms they would circulate. In a capitalist system, in contrast, accumulation is fueled by competition among private owners and producers, while society's resources are valued according to the determinates of market exchange.

---

14   R. Bellah, R. Madsen, W. Sullivan, A. Swidler and S. Tipton, *Habits of the Heart: Individualism and Commitment in American Life* (Berkeley: University of California Press, 1985); R. Putnam, *Bowling Alone: The Collapse and Revival of American Community* (New York: Simon and Schuster, 2000); R. Wuthnow, *Acts of Compassion: Caring for Others and Helping Ourselves* (Princeton: Princeton University Press, 1991).

The production and exchange of goods as well as the reproduction of society and its institutions appear to emerge spontaneously out of individuals' free transactions and interactions with each other and with the things that surround them.

How we behave in this system is for the most part a reflection of our urges and intentions rather than our considered compliance with externally imposed authority. This is what is usually meant by the ideal of individual freedom.[15] Yet such freedom is highly ambiguous and limited insofar as we have no real say over what kinds of things are produced and no control over the structures and institutions—like the market and its auxiliaries—through which we might express our tastes and desires. Nor can we shape the social relations or guide the economic trends that these structures generate. Free as we are to express ourselves, our power to exercise this freedom in socially meaningful ways is limited.

Values are a distinct kind of morality, different from, say, a sense of duty or a personal virtue, in that they mirror this powerless freedom. Unconstrained by external dictates and devoid of predetermined contents, values manifest a freedom of choice. They can be taken up or discarded, kept vague or left inactive. It is, moreover, the choice between different values that makes us experience our freedom most deeply.[16] But values are also free of the obligation to realize them: they can be asserted even when devoid of content and consequence. We can always claim to be moved by values rather than interests

---

15   L. Goldmann, *The Philosophy of the Enlightenment*, trans. H. Maas (London: Routledge, 1973); R. Williams, *Keywords* (London: Fontana, 1976).

16   J. Robbins, "Between Reproduction and Freedom: Morality, Value, and Radical Cultural Change," *Ethnos*, 2007, 72(3), 293–314.

without further ado, and we can assert values even when they are inactive, overridden by other considerations or unlikely to produce their projected outcomes. This is what inspired Friedrich Nietzsche to reevaluate values so damningly. In their self-exclusion from hostile reality, he wrote, values "reek of impotence."[17]

Two additional features make values distinct. The first is that they are not entirely subjective but presuppose a moral community that would recognize them as meaningful. They foreground the existence of like-minded others when they are grouped into national values, religious values, professional values, liberal values and so on. The second is that we normally claim values in opposition to self-interests. Indeed, we take values seriously, our own as well as those of others, only if they indicate disinterest. Values imply transcendence over desires: doing the right thing despite the temptation to act in self-serving ways.

Taken together, these attributes make values attractive to us as expressions of freedom and morality when our daily routines imply nothing of the sort. Responding to the pressure of competition over resources made scarce, we find ourselves preoccupied with private and pragmatic pursuits. We envision our investments bearing fruit, but this expectation runs the risk that our best efforts backfire. Even with the means to do well in our pursuits, we are bound to notice many situations in which we expend more than we receive and are held accountable for more than what we can control.

---

17   F. Nietzsche, "On the Genealogy of Morals," in W. Kaufman, ed., *Basic Writings of Nietzsche* (New York: The Modern Library, 1992 [1887]), 482.

Too many failures cannot but give rise to self-doubt and frustration. It is not our freedom that we experience most readily in these cases, but all the ways in which we are kicked around by circumstances.

If we nevertheless exert a measure of influence over our surroundings, along with other people similarly disposed, we can chafe against these circumstances through less disillusioning and more elevated forms of expression than self-concerned pragmatism. Chief among them are values. When asserting ourselves through values, we tread on steadier ground because values are anchored in convictions rather than realities, in the renunciation of material rewards and in a generality that is validated by the virtual existence of like-minded others without being beholden to their actual influence. In protests, volunteering, acts of solidarity and activism, values provide us with a compelling outlet for our fragile sense of power. They also assert our sense of freedom by making our unrewarded investments look like willing sacrifices. We seem to be transcending pragmatism for the sake of higher, immaterial ideals. Values thereby reconcile us with the rigidity of the structures that organize our lives. They allow us to rise above them in our imagination while making limited adjustments within the confines of what is possible to bend and modify. They give us a feeling that society does, to some extent, respond to our combined powers.

This is deftly illustrated in Nina Eliasoph's ethnography of civic groups in the United States.[18] She studied, among others, a regular peace vigil to block US arms shipments to

---

18   N. Eliasoph, *Avoiding Politics: How Americans Produce Apathy in Everyday Life* (Cambridge: Cambridge University Press, 1998).

other countries and a group trying to prevent a toxic incinerator from being built in their town. These activists and volunteers were united in their resolve to fight social injustices, in imagining a better society and in striving to turn this fantasy into reality. They organized protests, circulated petitions, lobbied and volunteered. Yet they remained insecure about their influence and suspicious of other people's motivations. This made them recast their goals as "close to home" issues that everyone should pursue out of self-interest and concern for their own children. As time wore on, their undertakings grew smaller and more feasible. The activists felt that worrying about problems they could not really solve was a waste of time and aimed instead at creating a corner of the world in which everyone could feel important and effective. Values gave credible outlet to their desire for self-determination, just as they were overwhelmed by predicaments beyond their reach.[19]

The US is perhaps an extreme example given the extent to which its economic policies have disempowered the working population. Germany offers a good contrast because its so-called social market economy has so far upheld social protections that Americans no longer enjoy, with industry-wide structures of negotiation between capital and labor

19 This resonated with my study of volunteers in Israel, whose activities depended on funds and a clientele by whose virtue they could bid for contracts, solicit budgets and attract free labor. Successful were those who scaled down their operations: specializing and marketing their added value as filling gaps in social provisioning. Moved to respond to urgent needs unmet by the government, they sought opportunities to do good in a society where the underprivileged depend on the generosity of the privileged: H. Weiss, "Gift and Value in Jerusalem's Third Sector," *American* Anthropologist, 2011, 113(4), 594–605.

rewarding wage-restraint with expansion of social policy.[20] After the Second World War, Germany set out to rebuild its middle class as part of a return to political consent. West Germany was reconstituted as a meritocratic open society, an ideal that was (unevenly) expanded eastward following Reunification. The broadness of Germany's middle class was debated in the 1980s in terms of the "two thirds society" of which it was said to comprise.[21] Its credibility relied on high standards of living that included even manual workers to the extent that Germany could boast a blurring of the collar line.[22]

Anthropologists have shed light on the ideologies animating this framework. Douglas Holmes looked at efforts by the German Central Bank to keep inflation at a steady low and maintain price stability. Bank officials translated these goals into guidelines for budgets, employment and commercial interest rates. They opposed wage- and price-setting attempts that would threaten the soundness of the German currency on the basis of "a broader story about the German state and its ability to manage the future by aligning its citizens' expectations with national interests."[23] Edward Fischer tracked the postulated confluence of interests among people he identified as middle-class shoppers. He saw it manifested in their readiness to assume personal

---

20 W. Plumpe, *German Economic and Business History in the Nineteenth and Twentieth Century* (New York: Palgrave Macmillan, 2016).

21 Social Democrat Peter Glotz first used this concept in his 1984 book *Die Arbeit der Zuspitzung*.

22 H. Siegrist, "From Divergence to Convergence: The Divided German Middle Class, 1945–2000," in O. Zunz, L. Schoppa and N. Hiwatari, eds., *Social Contracts under Stress: The Middle Classes of America, Europe and Japan at the Turn of the Century* (New York: Russell Sage Foundation, 2002).

23 D. R. Holmes, *Economy of Words: Communicative Imperatives in Central Banks* (Chicago: University of Chicago Press, 2014), 65.

responsibility over society, animals and the environment—in
whose welfare they saw a reflection of their own—by paying
higher prices for organic eggs and other "ethical products."[24]

Eggs also came up in my own observations of less affluent
Germans, namely a group of single mothers who convened to
get financial advice. The advisor spoke highly of the rights
to which Germany's social insurance entitled them, but she also
reminded them of their obligations. To drive the point home, she
told them about her widowed Bavarian aunts. Tante Hildegard
never worked, and her husband speculated with his business
earnings. Their value did not grow and Tante Hildegard ended
up struggling. Tante Greta's husband was an alcoholic who only
worked sporadically. She had to work too, then, and paid into
the public pension system. Well, guess who ended up sending
Tante Hildegard two dozen eggs each month? None other than
Tante Greta, proud of the money she earned for her retirement.
Warning the women against reliance on family or financial markets, the advisor concluded: "As soon as you manage to, get back
to work and pay your pension."

Political consent is solicited though the institutionally
anchored promise of security for those who invest, German-
style: work as much as they can, entrust the management of
their savings to the national economy, refrain from making
excessive demands upon it and pay out of pocket for morally
palatable products. Such an investment ethos must now be
asserted more forcefully for not bearing the fruit that much
of the population expects of it. Work in Germany is growing
more precarious and less rewarding, the living standards to

---

24   E. T. Fischer, *The Good Life: Aspiration, Dignity, and the Anthropology
of Wellbeing* (Stanford: Stanford University Press, 2014).

which Germans had grown accustomed are becoming more difficult to sustain, pension entitlements are coming under threat, while poverty and disaffection are on the rise. My most recent research on financial advice tracked the subsequent political and moral stirrings.

In the face of lackadaisical attitudes toward finance on the part of clients, I noticed that advisers would harp on people's responsibilities toward their children and on family values more generally. They recommended that parents give children allowances to teach them how to manage their money and advised them to resist their children's excessive demands while opening long-term savings accounts for each child. They endorsed real estate investment on the principle that it would give families long-term stability and that the property would eventually form a nice inheritance. And they urged everyone to pay off their debts and save sufficiently for old age so as not to become a burden on their grown children.

Financial advisors also valorized personal responsibility. This morality—which pervades public discourse in Germany—consists of working hard and saving vigilantly, being scrupulous about consumption, taking on only those debts that one can service to maturity, keeping a balanced budget and provisioning for the future. What one lacks in self-discipline may be corrected by the nudges of the market, for example with automatic deductions out of paychecks, tax discounts on money invested in sanctioned ways, and the assumption of feasible repayment commitments for durable property. One cannot spend money needlessly, it is reasoned, if this money is already pledged toward a greater good.

Such responsibility is the counterpart of the country's fiscal austerity. Presented by its political and economic leadership as a backbone of citizenship, it is often expressed in contrast to the supposed moral shortcomings of indebted countries like Greece. But this morality has come under strain now that German savers are losing money on their savings because of low interest rates and are being warned that their pension savings will not suffice to uphold their living standards upon retirement. Accustomed to saving responsibly while having their banks and social insurance safeguard the value of their savings, many Germans assume this arrangement to be ongoing. They are less excited about being addressed solely as consumers of risky financial products.

Advisors remind economically weaker populations of their social security entitlements, urge them to work and save responsibly, and warn them against overspending and indebtedness. They teach populations with greater resources how to use their financial assets to their advantage, for example by investing in real estate or in globally diversified stock or index funds whose revenues could outstrip inflation. They sometimes show graphs depicting stock growth over the past half century or so. In these graphs, dramatic political events as well as economic upswings and downturns effectuate tiny leaps and slumps, quickly smoothed over by a general upward trend. Wars, election results, crises and natural disasters feature solely as triggers of short-term volatility.

Clients and audiences express concern over the political and moral repercussions of these products, but their concerns are contained within the bounds of the newly financialized investment ethos. In one seminar on long-term saving, an advisor projected a slide showing how the value of stock has grown over time. When attendees brought up ethics and ecology, she responded by naming a couple of financial products that invest in "clean" enterprise, but reminded them that these products are part of the same market. Pointing to the screen, she urged: "Look again and you will see that despite the volatility, the lines go up. The economy grows: it's a reflection of that. You may not like this trend but it is the only economy we have. Our only choice is to join it." Joining the market—the only reasonable option presented to German consumers—blunts the politic edge of their grievances.[25] Their national market offers them some protections at the price of self-imposed austerity, while global finance channels their fears toward products and strategies that promote accumulation.

Alternatives are even more limited in countries with fewer protections. In Israel, public safety nets and support for work and post-work incomes are far stingier than Germany's, while the cost of living is higher. The pressures this places on workers came to a head with the political uprising of the summer of 2011. In a country where national security almost always takes center stage, mass mobilization against economic difficulties was a breathtaking drama. Yet, despite the size and scale of the protests, propelled by a backwind of media support, and despite their early endorsement by mainstream politicians and a government quick to form committees charged with finding solutions to protestors' complaints, the cost of living in Israel had not been lowered. In particular the cost of housing—the uprising's flagship cause—continues to escalate and burden home buyers with decades of debt.

---

25 So also with German gentrifiers who voice concerns over social sustainability, justice and cohesion but respond pragmatically to "circumstances" of urban employment and parenting; per S. Frank and S. Weck, "Being Good Parents or Being Good Citizens," *International Journal of Urban and Regional Research* 2018, 42(1), 20–35.

Sociologists Zeev Rosenhek and Michael Shalev have interpreted the protests as a reflection of middle-class decline: the eroding life chances of young adults whose parents had benefited from the liberalization of Israel's economy.[26] From its inception, the Israeli state has overseen the construction of a wide-reaching bureaucratic and professional apparatus, including an industrial sector and a banking system, which have allowed Israel's veteran (Ashkenazi Jewish) population to secure advantages in the job market and to amass resources. Welfare arrangements and subsidies helped them acquire academic degrees, attain relatively high-paying positions and purchase homes. But recent decades have seen the devaluation of work and withdrawal of public resources, making it very hard for their children to reach for the same advantages. In the protests, they articulated their demands in terms of social justice and national interest. But according to Rosenhek and Shalev, large segments of the Israeli population lacked the parental endowments and human capital that these protesters had and so could not have shared their desire to have their investments count.

As the dust settled on the uprising, and its failure to lower housing costs became evident, I set about my own study, interviewing professionals in the housing market, sitting in on mortgage transactions, attending meetings by home-buyers' groups and talking to young adults seeking homes. What I discovered was the urgency with which protestors and their cohorts were pushed to safeguard their future. In public discourse, they were labeled "middle class" for their sheer ability to buy a home with a mortgage. Their investments in real estate predisposed them toward market solutions to their plight. They distrusted political interventions that might favor one constituency over another, unless the constituency favored was that of working and tax-paying military veterans, which in Israel is coded language for the middle class.[27]

The rental market in Israel is virtually unregulated. Anyone who wants to give their children a modicum of stability cannot afford to move to a new apartment every couple of years on account of their landlords' decision to raise the rent or sell the house. Buying a home is therefore of paramount importance. The circumstances of first-time home buyers, namely meager savings and modest salaries, force them to seek maximal financing for minimal monthly repayments. These loans end up being the most expensive, adding up over decades through interest and fees. The image propagated in the media, of young adults shrewdly investing in real estate in the anticipation of rising prices, is nevertheless an easy sell. It seems to vindicate the extravagant costs of homes bought with thirty-year mortgages, compelling home buyers to operate as de facto investors until middle age. By dignifying necessity as personal choice, it puts a positive spin on expenses that make little economic sense.

Homeownership is valued above rent, which goes into someone else's pocket. First-time home buyers I spoke with, all of whom had some experience in the rental market, never failed to mention this. They would rather put money into something of

27 It excludes Israel's ultraorthodox and Palestinian citizens, most of whom cannot compete over the same resources, as well as the poorest populations, who lack basic resources for investment and social mobility.

their own than give the same amount to someone else. They did not bother calculating how much they would end up paying for their home after their mortgage was repaid in full, nor did they keep track of its market value. "Even if I sell my apartment today, what apartment could I afford instead?" was a common reply to my questions. Instead, they considered the relative advantages of living in their own home. Struggling to make it in a society of landlords and tenants, no price was too high. Today's overpriced home might fall out of reach tomorrow, and so they strove to get on the first rung of the real estate ladder as early as possible.

The predicament of young adults in Israel with eroding life chances—the very people who had united to protest the cost of living and housing—has effectively collapsed into inter-household competition. Successive generations of each household now pool their resources to maintain and reproduce their advantages. Parents pledge what resources they have to helping their grown kids purchase homes of their own. Young adults avail themselves of this help, which they leverage with bank financing, for the sake of their own children. The urgency of creating this kind of security for their families discourages them from prioritizing their common grievances.

Instead, they relate to one another as the satisfactory neighbors whose presence might bolster the value of the homes they bought; as the peers whose prior home purchases troublingly drive up the cost of housing, or whose subsequent purchases help inflate home values; and as the landlords to whom rent paid amounts to money thrown away. Begrudgingly, they ally themselves with the banks that leverage their investment through long-term loans, as well as with government institutions charged with protecting the value of their purchases and of their parents' and teachers' investments in their future.

These crosscutting competitions and coalitions generate the social fragmentation that makes sustained political struggle all but impossible.

The stories I have told in this chapter are meant to demonstrate the self-defeating nature of the politics and values that flourish among those who subscribe to a middle-class ideology of investment-driven self-determination. Capitalism severs workers from non market sources of livelihood and makes them compete over things as crucial as jobs, housing and education. It keeps these resources scarce to maintain high profit rates while compelling workers to act in self-serving ways to preserve what they have and reach for more. At the same time, it inspires in them a sense of personal freedom, bolstered by the investments they are encouraged to make.

Emboldened by this freedom, investing workers confront injustices too glaring to ignore. These injustices elicit responses among those with the means to rise above the daily grind. But their values bespeak powerlessness, and their politics are handicapped by entanglement with material pressures and incentives. The outcomes of their activism, whether geared toward securing a decent living for everyone or toward the protection of their own investments, reproduce collective vulnerability and disadvantage. The greater the common insecurity and the fiercer the competitive pressures, the more plausible these actions and values nevertheless appear. Hence, to circle back to Max Horkheimer, "the overcoming of this morality lies not in the positing of a better one, but in the creation of conditions under which their reason for existing is eliminated."[28]

---

28 M. Horkheimer, "Egoism and Freedom Movements: On the Anthropology of the Bourgeois Era," 57.

Conclusion

Our actions don't always have the significance we intend. We like to think of them as free and consequential, but our considerations when making them, no less than their practical reverberations, are prescribed within structures governed by dynamics and directionalities at variance with our own. By examining connections between institutions, practices and beliefs, anthropology alerts us to such discrepancies and can help us trace how they relate to each other. Such an approach is particularly well suited for the study of the so-called middle class. The designation defines capitalism's protagonists: workers who contribute to accumulation not only through their work but also through their willing sacrifices in other domains. Investing more time, effort and material resources than the immediate satisfaction of their desires would necessitate, and doing so for the sake of their well-being in the future, workers are ordained self-determining actors. This holds true even as their investments are in response to external pressures, and when the outcomes of these investments undermine the goals they were meant to accomplish.

Such paradox provoked a forerunner of critical theory: Hungarian philosopher Georg Lukács's groundbreaking essay from 1923, "Reification and the Consciousness of the Proletariat."[1] Its aim was to uncover opportunities for proletarian revolt, but Lukács spent the greater part of it dissecting the culture and thought of the bourgeoisie. He drew on Marx's analysis of capitalism as a system that denies people independent and collective means of livelihood. Its institutions are designed, not to satisfy people's needs and desires but to regulate their efforts to sustain their households through market-mediated work and consumption, in a way that fuels accumulation. In their daily exchanges, people's considerations are guided by the way things are socially valued. These values are determined by the average work time necessary to produce the commodities and services they seek. The variables that factor into the valuation of these goods are perennially reset when work and investments, along with the technologies that enable them and the politics that support or contest them, combine to reconfigure standards of productivity. The stuff of everyday life under capitalism is therefore a constellation of mutually adjusting influences in a global production process oriented toward the accumulation of a surplus. It strings all political, economic, legal and social institutions together to comprise what Lukács called a totality.

---

1   G. Lukács, "Reification and the Consciousness of the Proletariat," in *History and Class Consciousness*, 83–222, trans. R. Livingstone (Cambridge, MA: MIT Press, 2002 [1923]).

This totality stands in stark opposition to the immediacy with which capitalism compels everyone to operate: people's isolation in the narrow confines of their everyday lives and the mundane pressures and incentives they confront in their activities. Scholars, too, are trapped in immediacy and have no choice but to theorize from its standpoint. Their observations grant them access, therefore, to mere fragments of totality. And yet they tend to build outward from these fragments as though they were independently real and universally significant. Lukács analyzed the foundations of modern ontology, ethics and aesthetics as examples of the attitudes that the entrapment in immediacy brings about. Sophisticated generalizations grant institutions, attitudes and relations specific to capitalism the appearance of being reality pure and simple.

He argued that the fragmented positioning of individual thought and action vis-à-vis totality brings about conformity. People contemplate their surroundings as if they are what they are by necessity. They reserve their energy for specializing and strategizing within the structures that absorb their attention, perpetuating them with their focused activities. They measure and model the possibilities and impacts of their action, classifying those that fail to match up with their calculations as idiosyncrasies and sources of error. They take advantage of the opportunities that their social positions make available to them and they view these opportunities in a light that complements their pursuits. In thrall to the facts as they find them, even their moral values end up being quietist instantiations of formalism, impartiality and pragmatism.

Lukács considered these attitudes most deeply entrenched among the bourgeoisie, because their prospects are tied up with their self-interests. Interests can be described as internalizations of the material limitations and incentives that support accumulation. They are manifested as an orientation to the rewards entailed in the specific roles that people occupy. People with awareness of their interests are poised to avail themselves of the opportunities that come with their position and avoid actions that threaten to set them back. If the advantages they gain are proportional to the efforts they have exerted, these fortunes seem to emanate exclusively from this pursuit of their interests. People's positions in totality dictate the conditions that make their investments possible, as well as their likely outcomes. Yet the entrancement of interests obscures totality in its gradations and imbroglios. The rewards for pursuing interests and the penalties for not doing so stimulate ongoing investments. They also grant investors a sense of agency and control. As Lukács put it, the bourgeoisie harbor the illusion that they are in command of their lives because they are imprisoned by their self-interests.[2]

Lukács wrote his essay with the proletariat in mind, believing that if workers were to discover the sources of their exploitation they would resist it. He considered this impossible for the bourgeoisie because of the seductiveness of their interests. They are afforded privileged opportunities to pursue their interests, and the satisfaction of tracing their advantages back to having done so successfully. Consciousness of their foundations would therefore be tantamount to suicide for the bourgeoisie, in that they cohere as a class around self-interest. Social democracy was therefore a huge problem for Lukács: he

---

2   G. Lukács, "Reification and the Consciousness of the Proletariat," 163–64.

feared its capacity to forge common interests between workers and the bourgeoisie, bringing even the most intransigent elements of society into capitalism's fold. As indeed it has, becoming a major propagator of an expansive middle-class ideology that encompasses the divisive proletariat and bourgeoisie classifications of old.

In this book, I revisited the themes that preoccupied Lukács by proceeding along a different path. I proposed that the middle class is an ideology of investment-driven self-determination, assigned to and largely embraced by workers with the means to invest extra work, time and other resources for the sake of their well-being in the future, rather than using everything up on the immediate satisfaction of their desires. The ideology is generated by and serves a capitalist system that feeds on people's investments while not affirming them in the self-determining way it suggests. This is because capitalism reproduces itself through an accumulation process that elicits ever more physical and material resources out of people who, in aggregate, are not fully remunerated for these investments, cannot opt out of making them without paying a formidable price, and are unable to steer their lives in a course that transcends the isolation and competition this elicitation imposes upon them. Their isolation and competition compel them to repeat the same behaviors over and over again and thereby reproduce the structure that entraps them.

To establish this argument, I took a closer look at some of the institutions in which the middle-class ideology is implicated, and highlighted contradictions in the practices they inspire. I interrogated property, broadly conceived to include privately owned homes, savings accounts, stocks and bonds, insurance policies and other material and immaterial assets. My aim was to show how what seems to be a universal means of meeting our possessive inclinations and storing the value of our investments is actually a construct designed to reconcile us, insofar as the value of our work is never fully remunerated, with our exploitation; and to encourage us, for the sake of owning what we imagine to be value-storing and -enhancing resources, to invest more than we would otherwise be prepared to. I went on to interrogate human capital, including cultural, educational and professional tastes, skills, credentials and networks. My aim was to show how a category that reflects skills, tastes and connections is designed to make us believe that we are investors of personal powers that emerge out of our prior investments. It is also designed to spur us, for the sake of creating and maintaining the advantages necessary to get ahead in life rather than fall behind, to never cease investing. I also traced the pressures that human capital puts on family bonds. I then turned to the politics associated with the middle class. My aim was to demonstrate some ways in which competitive investment undermines the goals it sets out to accomplish. As part of this exploration, I looked at the values that are designed in their disinterest, generality and inconsequentiality to assert our sense of freedom and agency, just as our political powers are curtailed.

The red thread running through these lines of inquiry is investment, and it is the beating heart of the middle-class ideology. Nowadays, representatives of the finance sector endorse the idea of investment most vocally. They pronounce that we ought to be savvy financial actors who, instead of losing money by letting it languish in a bank account where its value will be eroded by inflation, should invest it in global finance, exploiting risks for profit and diversifying to ride the waves of market volatility. Investment also pervades everyday language as a metaphor through which we articulate a diverse array of relations and choices. It captures our imagination because of how capacious it is, both socially, as people worldwide are encouraged to strategize as investors, and practically, as we conceive of our nonfinancial activities like education, skill building and socializing as investments.

Investment can be thought of as forfeiture in the present of more work, time, money or emotional resources than those whose fruits can immediately be consumed. It is motivated by the anticipation that their equivalents will be retrieved sometime in the future. Expected rewards may take on a range of forms, so long as they are of identical value to what was invested or include added value that represents the growth to which the invested value has contributed, granting some risk of backfire. As correlate to this conservative estimate, investment presumes continuity, coherence and predictability: linking present actions to future outcomes. It suggests a sequence in which value flows through material objects, savings deposits, credentials and social relations toward identical or greater values. And it suggests personal powers: the value realized at the end of the investment is believed to be an outcome of the effort and initiative that had originally set the process in motion. It further implies that the property, human capital or social relations invested in are durable. Their durability, in turn, depends on these objects and relations being rooted in a relatively stable system that allows them to store the value invested in them and that permits this value to be converted at will to its equivalents.[3]

---

3 So central is investment to the middle-class ideology that among the most salient ways of identifying non-middle-class populations in poor

So understood, investment is untenable under the dominance of finance and its insinuation into the reproduction of families, societies and political institutions. Financialization makes values, their repositories and the market forces that reconfigure them too unstable for investments to yield predictable outcomes or to always be convertible to their equivalents. Novel financial instruments allow professional investors to profit whether asset values go up or down, exacerbating market volatility and weakening the ability of property and assets to act as safe repositories for the value placed into them. At the same time, credit cards, student loans, mortgages, deductions and installments help everyone enjoy investment targets now while promising to pay for them in the future, or to pay piecemeal for things they only partly own or will possibly never fully attain, effectively collapsing investment and outcome.

The notion of investment chimes with ideas about planning for the future. Economists (from Franco Modigliani and Richard Brumberg in the 1950s through many subsequent developments) have modeled the rationality and foresight of

countries or at the margins of rich ones is by their distance from this ideal. Anthropologists like Richard Wilk, "Consumer Culture and Extractive Industry on the Margins of the World System," in J. Brewer and F. Trentmann, eds., *Consumer Cultures: Global Perspectives* (Oxford: Berg, 2006); Richard Wilk, "The Extractive Economy: An Early Phase of the Globalization of Diet, and Its Environmental Consequences," in A. Hornborg, J. McNeil and J. Martinez-Alier, eds., *Rethinking Environmental History: World System History and Global Environmental Change* (Lanham, MD: AltaMira Press, 2007); and those contributing to a volume edited by S. Day, E. Papataxiarchis and M. Stewart, eds., *Lilies of the Field* (Boulder, CO: Westview Press, 1999), discuss day laborers, gypsies, prostitutes and vagrants as binging rather than storing things for the future and as living fully in the present; although see J. Guyer, "Further: A Rejoinder," *American Ethnologist*, 2007, 34(3), 449, for a rebuttal of the idea that this is a class attribute.

saving, spending and investing with the conventional life course in mind. In anticipation of a gradual rise in our work earnings at adulthood and their termination upon retirement, these models have us as trying to maintain or improve our living standards by advancing capital for education and skill building when we are young, using our earnings as working adults to build up reserves in a home and a pension, and spending these reserves on the things that we need when retired.

In the post–Second World War era, risk-pooling arrangements and other regulations of national economies in rich parts of the world have, for a while, granted some plausibility to this kind of planning. But the current unpredictability of work incomes and investment outcomes (or, as these predicaments are respectively glossed, precarity and volatility) makes life-course planning far less tenable. Still, it continues to hold sway in the context of a middle-class ideology, where life's milestones are construed in terms of investment. This applies to education, homeownership, careers and pension savings, as well as to conjugality, childbirth and parenthood, and the forging and maintaining of social relationships. Investments in them are deemed middle-class rites of passage and normative features of adulthood, family life, sociability and retirement.

Investment makes it seem as though the value of our savings and material assets (like a home) or immaterial assets (like an academic degree), often purchased through credit, installment plans or insurance deductions, is somehow preserved and accessible to us whenever we need it. It prioritizes them over other, collective strategies through which we could conceivably determine our fortunes. It casts us in the role of forward-looking agents who willingly store our resources in durable repositories or entrust them to banks and other intermediaries charged with

preserving their value or making it grow, where in fact investments are extracted from us by necessity. In understanding
ourselves to be self-determining investors, we unwittingly side
with the forces of surplus accumulation. This, insofar as we
derive most of our income from work whose value is not fully
remunerated, while assuming responsibility over the diminished
value of our work and investments.

Just as we sense the dusk of the middle class in reports about
its decline and squeeze, so we can perceive in these contradictions the twilight of investment, its ideational backbone. Those
of us owing mortgages on homes worth less than what we are
paying for them or facing a job market that does not reward the
human capital we have accrued are liable to ask ourselves why
we keep investing so much. Paul Willis encountered a similar
puzzle in his ethnographic study of social prospects being
recreated in the classroom.[4] Describing the school-time interactions of English working-class boys, he concluded that
despite education's conceit of leveling the playing field, these
boys were doomed through their extracurricular activities to
subordinate social positions. He then went on to describe the
conformism of schoolchildren identified as middle class.
Having invested in the formal aims of education, they sacrificed some of their autonomy to support school authorities.
Willis saw them and the people they would grow up to become
as going a step further in expecting school officials, as well as
those of the state, legal institutions and the police, to preserve
the rules above and beyond the call of duty.

It stands to reason that those who have something to gain
from the institutions that elicit their investments and safeguard

---

4   P. Willis, *Learning to Labour* (Burlington VT: Ashgate, 2012).

their value would also support these institutions. As I have explained in this book, institutions like private property and human capital harness private resources for capital accumulation through incentives. These incentives are internalized as self-interests because they are often rewarded, if only provisionally and in the form of relative advantage over others. But how to explain people's *excessive* investments and renunciations, of the kind they make when their efforts are not rewarded and when their interests are not served or even undermined? Willis's depiction is hardly outlandish. Many of us would sooner endure the punishment of insufficient rewards and backfired investments, indeed, subject ourselves to more of them, than question the value of investments we have already made. Recall that one of the conundrums that motivated this book was the vast over-representation of the middle class: the tendency of many more people to consider themselves middle class than would be so identified by any of the common measures, even as their investments do not win them the benefits they prefigure.

If that is the power of ideology, it runs very deep. So deep that father of psychoanalysis Sigmund Freud, noticing people's tendency to wallow in guilt and shame that are out of proportion to any wrongs they may have committed, deemed psychic excess endemic to modern life.[5] Affirming the diagnosis, critical theorist Herbert Marcuse claimed that Freud misrecognized its sources.[6] Rather than emerging out of a universal clash between our innermost desires and the demands of civilized

5   S. Freud, *Civilization and Its Discontents* (New York: W. W. Norton & Company, 1989).

6   H. Marcuse, *Eros and Civilization: A Philosophical Inquiry into Freud* (Boston, MA: Beacon Press, 1974).

society, as Freud had it, psychic excess replicates a historically specific socioeconomic excess: the pressure imposed on work, investments and the institutions that coordinate them to produce more value than the value retrieved from them. Excess, according to Marcuse, is just another word for surplus. We cannot be healed of it insofar as it mirrors, deep within our psyche, the excessive investments that capitalist accumulation forces us to make in order to earn a living, feed our families and carve out our fortunes.

If we invest too much, then, and support thereby the structures and institutions that elicit our investments, we are essentially responding to pressures and incentives. And if in the process we affirm the sense of investment-driven self-determination, we are glorifying this response as free choice. The self-determination implied by the middle class is false. However much we endeavor to chart the course of our lives, the structures that coordinate our practices and relationships are designed to promote goals that are at odds with the satisfaction of our desires, the realization of our dreams and the dispelling of our fears. They pit us against each other in competition over advantages and against disadvantages, while bringing us together in provisional and instrumental alliances to protect the value of our investments. The competition that capitalism enforces robs us of the ability to organize durably and effectively in movements that transcend it.

But contradictions are not only sources of frustration. They also allow us to think more clearly and to be less taken in by appearances—ultimately, to manipulate the tensions they give rise to in ways that might lead to genuine transformation. Contradictions stimulate our powers of reflection while also gaining clarity through these powers. We are not dupes who mindlessly follow the dictates of the structures in which we are imprisoned and who unquestioningly subscribe to the ideologies that permeate our societies. Introducing friction into operations programmed to proceed smoothly, contradictions provoke among us a critical appraisal of what we do and why we do it. Disillusionment with the ideal of self-determination is an opportunity to create the conditions for it to actually be fulfilled. We can genuinely govern our lives if we manage to transform social structures and institutions into ones more responsive to our combined wills and powers. We can reflect, criticize and act collectively toward a society that manifests our intentions and nurtures our powers, because that is who we have always been.

Index